Using the New In Chess app is easy!

■ get early access to every issue
■ replay all games in the Gameviewer

1

Sign in with your username and
password to access the digital issue.

2

Read the article, optimized
for your screen size.

3

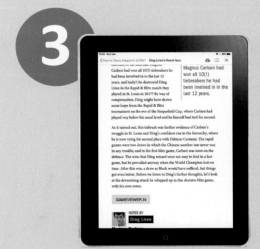

Click on the Gameviewer button
to get to the built-in chess board.

4

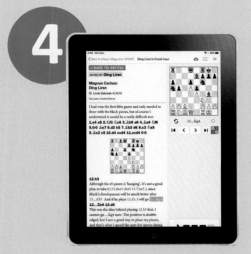

Replay the game, including an option
to analyze with Stockfish.

The only chess magazine that moves
www.newinchess.com/chess-apps – for tablet, phone and PC

‹O› Meltwater
CHAMPIONS CHESS TOUR
2021

The **New In Chess Classic** starts on April 24!

REGULAR	MAJOR	REGULAR	MAJOR
SKILLING OPEN	**AIRTHINGS MASTERS**	**OPERA EURO RAPID**	**MAGNUS CARLSEN INVITATIONAL**
Nov 22 - Nov 30	Dec 26 - Jan 3	Feb 6 - Feb 14	Mar 13 - Mar 21

NEXT UP!

REGULAR	MAJOR	REGULAR	REGULAR
NEW IN CHESS CLASSIC	**TOURNAMENT #6**	**TOURNAMENT #7**	**TOURNAMENT #8**
Apr 24 - May 2	May 23 - May 31	Jun 26 - Jul 4	Jul 31 - Aug 8

REGULAR	
TOURNAMENT #9	**FINAL**
Aug 28 - Sep 5	Sep 25 - Oct 3

Find out more at **championschesstour.com**

2021#3

NEW IN CHESS

3

Contents

'The queen is the most powerful piece even if the king gets all the attention.'

CONTRIBUTORS TO THIS ISSUE
Levon Aronian, Maxim Dlugy, Jorden van Foreest, Anish Giri, John Henderson, Davorin Kuljasevic, Noam Manella, Bruce Monson, Peter Heine Nielsen, Maxim Notkin, Judit Polgar, Matthew Sadler, Han Schut, Kaja Snare, Wesley So, Jonathan Tisdall, Thomas Willemze

Peak Performance

Many would believe that Alexander Riazantsev reached his peak performance when he captured the 2016 Russian championship title. But not so, it appears, as the popular Russian grandmaster and coach reached another 'peak performance'. Only this time it was playing chess at the top of Mount Kilimanjaro's Uhuru Peak. Riazantsev is a keen mountaineer, and in early March he brought the game to new heights by climbing and playing above the clouds at its summit. At 5,895 metres above sea level, Uhuru Peak is the world's tallest free-standing mountain, and this is the first time chess has been played there. His opponent was Rashid, his Kilimanjaro National Park guide, whom he diplomatically agreed a quick draw to.

Originally Riazantsev's expedition to Mount Kilimanjaro was scheduled for April 2020 together with Daniil Dubov, whose trainer he has been in the past years. But a week before their departure date, the trip had to be cancelled because of the coronavirus pandemic. Unfortunately, Dubov was unable to join his coach for the re-arranged date.

Uhuru Peak is the latest of Riazantsev's conquests, having already climbed the highest mountain in Europe and Russia, Mount Elbrus (5,642 meters), Mount Kazbek (5,033 meters) in the Georgia Caucasus, and 'Razdelnaya' (6,148 meters), one of the seven peaks in the Pamir mountain range in the Himalayas that spans Central Asia, South Asia, and East Asia. ∎

It's Carson v Fischer!

It's amazing the nostalgic gems that get uploaded from time to time on YouTube. One new posting that certainly caught our attention was a fascinating, near 19-minute appearance by newly-crowned World Champion Bobby

Johnny Carson cannot believe his eyes as brand-new chess World Champion Bobby Fischer solves the '15 Puzzle' in just 23 seconds.

Fischer on 'The Tonight Show' with Johnny Carson, that originally aired on 8 November, 1972.

Carson was the legendary 'King of Late Night TV' and an appearance on his show meant you really had made the celebrity A-list. Both Carson and Fischer were on sparkling form throughout the lively interview, which mixed fact with fun, as was the host's interview style. Carson's opening gambit was to ask how Fischer felt immediately after he'd won the title, to which Fischer admitted it all felt a little like a letdown: 'I woke up the day after the thing was over, and I just felt different – like something had been taken out of me.'

Fischer also chips in: 'This is the big problem, how I top it', and then with perfect television timing and a big smile on his face, adds: 'But I figure if I can keep the title for about 30 years, something like that.' Explaining to the host that his title defence wouldn't be until 1975, Carson asks Fischer what his plans would be till then. 'I like to play', comes the ironic

reply from the man who abdicated his title. 'What am I gonna do for three years? I can't do talk shows just for three years!'

The big fun moment came near the end when Carson decided to test Fischer's IQ by asking him to solve a '15 Puzzle', the fabled sliding tile puzzle of the time with numbered squares in random order with one tile missing. Fischer aced it. 'That's how I got interested in chess – because I was playing all the other games and they just were too easy', came the reply as he solved it in just 23 seconds. He then teasingly added 'They didn't mix it up too well', to which Carson sardonically smiled and revealed he was the one who scrambled it!

Dancing Queen?

Following hard on the heels of Anya Taylor-Joy's Golden Globe award for her role in Netflix smash hit *The Queen's Gambit* comes another major accolade for the young actress. In early April, the American-born Argentine-British multi-talent also picked up the best female actor award in a TV Movie or Limited Series category at the 27th annual Screen Actors Guild (SAG).

What will be next for cultural juggernaut Beth Harmon? While many have speculated on a follow-up second series from the streaming giant following their global success of the plucky orphan girl and chess prodigy, it looks more likely that she

Anya Taylor-Joy is becoming a specialist in giving acceptance speeches from home.

could be set to become a dancing queen on the stage, with a musical adaptation of *The Queen's Gambit* now in the works.

The rights to Walter Tevis's 1983 novel were acquired by the New York production company Level Forward, which already has four big Broadway hits to its name. 'It is a privilege to lead the charge of bringing *The Queen's Gambit* to the stage through the beloved and enduring craft of musical theatre', said Level Forward CEO Adrienne Becker and producer Julia Dunetz in a statement. 'The story [of Beth Harmon] is a siren call amidst our contemporary struggles for gender and racial equity, and we're looking forward to moving the project forward.'

And the winner is...

And Anya isn't the only award-winning woman in chess. Women's World Rapid champion Humpy Koneru was genuinely surprised and overjoyed when it was announced

Humpy Koneru: Champion, Wife, Mother and Sportswoman of the Year!

during a live virtual ceremony in early March that she had won the BBC Indian Sportswoman of the Year title for 2020, following a public vote conducted by the global broadcaster.

The 33-year-old – who returned to tournament praxis in December 2019 following a two-year maternity break – beat off sprinter Dutee Chand, airgun shooter Manu Bhaker, wrestler Vinesh Phogat and India hockey captain Rani Rampal to claim the coveted award.

'Being an indoor game, chess doesn't get as much attention as sports like cricket get in India. But with this award, I hope the game will draw people's attention', she said after winning the honour. 'I won over the years because of my willpower and confidence. A female player should never think about quitting her game. Marriage and motherhood are just a part of our life and they should not change the course of our lives', she added.

Postal Chess

The German Deutsche Post AG service announced one for the collectors by issuing a special blue 110 cent stamp on 1 March to commemorate the 25th anniversary of the first winning game of IBM's Supercomputer Deep Blue in its first match against Garry Kasparov.

Those were the days, when the World Champion losing to a computer was frontpage news...

The historic moment that a computer beat a reigning World Champion for the first time (under classical tournament conditions) took place in the Philadelphia Convention Center on 10 February, 1996. Kasparov went on to triumph in the match by 4-2, but memorably he went on to defend the 'honour of mankind' in a rematch the following year in New York.

Kasparov sensationally lost that 'Man verses Machine' match to Deep Blue by 2½-3½ – and we look forward to next May to see if Deutsche Post AG will also commemorate the 25th anniversary of that even more momentous occasion, seen by

many as a big milestone moment in computer and software history.

Pride & Sorrow

Chess players and fans have been known to get all misty-eyed at the mention of 'opera' with it conjuring up thoughts of the most famous game of the great Paul Morphy. It was at the Paris Opera House – during a performance of Bellini's opera Norma – that the American wizard brilliantly beat aristocracy amateurs the Duke of Brunswick and Count Isouard in an offhand blindfold game played at the Paris Opera House in 1858.

Now there's even more reason to get sentimental, as that fabled game, not to mention Morphy's short, brilliant, yet ultimately tortured life, will be coming to a streaming service near you soon in *The Opera Game,* that inevitably will draw comparisons to Netflix's recent runaway chess hit.

'With *The Queen's Gambit*, the filmmakers are paying close attention to the chess', said producer/co-writer Ken Mask on the release of his movie. 'We are playing close attention to [Morphy's] life, instead of the next great chess move. We try to document what's happening in someone's life outside of what they're known for.'

The thoughtful and beautifully filmed 79-minute period piece

Here young Morphy is still feigning to read a book, but soon he will be playing chess too!

was directed by Spike Lee associate Monty Ross and co-written by Simeon Marsalis, son of jazz

musician Wynton Marsalis. The veteran film and stage actor, Clarke Peters of *The Wire* fame, also narrates this 'hidden figure' story that opens on the night of Morphy's untimely and mysterious death in post-Civil War New Orleans.

Love, Chess

New world No.8 Andrey Rublev is storming up the tennis ranking after a phenomenal 20-game winning streak, and four straight ATP 500 Tour titles after capturing the ABN AMRO World Tennis Tour-

Andrey Rublev plays chess like he plays tennis and vice versa.

nament in Rotterdam, Netherlands, in February. Did the young Russian credit a new coach for his strong start to 2021? Nope, it seems it had more to do with his love of chess!

Apart from being a hot property on the ATP Tour, Rublev is also a big chess fan, and ahead of a possible fifth straight title win in Dubai in early March, he told the media his prowess on the chessboard is the big reason for his success on the court. 'Chess can help tennis, maybe strategy-wise. It gives you more patience, but I play chess like I play tennis. I try and take a Queen, or a forehand in tennis, and dictate. I prepare to attack.'

Alas, Rublev's golden run on the ATP 500 Tour ground to a halt, as he lost in the semi-finals in Dubai to fellow Russian Aslan Karatsev, 2-6, 6-4, 4-6. ∎

Dutchman wins Magnus Carlsen Invitational

Giri reigns supreme

Despite a commanding performance, Magnus Carlsen finished yet another tournament without coming out on top. The undisputed star of the Magnus Carlsen Invitational was Anish Giri, who remained brilliant and resilient till the last day, when he shook off Ian Nepomniachtchi. As he celebrated, Giri tried not to be over-excited about his success. Carlsen would not have that: 'This is by far the biggest tournament that he has ever won.' **JONATHAN TISDALL** reports from Oslo.

Magnus Carlsen started these online rapid chess tours to fill a calendar ravaged by the Covid pandemic. The opening of the second season coincided with the World Champion's 30th birthday, and marked the beginning of an unprecedented drought of tournament victories for the Norwegian. With the fourth event of the Meltwater Champions Chess Tour bearing his name, his thirst for success would surely be higher than ever.

The Magnus Carlsen Invitational was the second 'Major' event of the tour, meaning that it had a fatter prize fund and guaranteed the winner a spot in the Tour Final. One slightly confusing aspect was that the MCI featured a field of 16 players, two via a qualifier, while the Major format was originally set as 12. Whether this shift in search of added excitement and audience interest will reappear in the third and final Major in late May remains to be determined.

The first of three five-round days began the process of whittling down the field by half for the knock-out segment. The fight for survival produced plenty of drama, and a few eyebrow-raising moments. Recent tour virtuoso Wesley So was shocked as White vs. Ian Nepomniachtchi in Round 1, and ended the day with a wobbly blunder vs. Giri for another White loss – but still a respectable 50% on a bad day.

Event host Carlsen looked strong and energetic, but was only tied for second with Levon Aronian after Anish Giri raced half a point ahead to 4/5, including a win over Magnus in their Round 4 meeting.

NOTES BY
Anish Giri

Anish Giri
Magnus Carlsen
Magnus Carlsen Invitational 2021
(prelims 4)
Sicilian Defence, Accelerated Dragon

In the Magnus Carlsen Invitational, I played a couple of very interesting games from a chess viewpoint, but in terms of the result, my win against the World Champion definitely stands out.
1.e4 c5 2.♘f3 g6
Magnus had already played this move, so it didn't come as a surprise. As I joked, I had sent my fellow-Dutchman Jorden van Foreest reconnoitring in the first round. He lost his game against Carlsen, but that told me where the enemy's defence forces were – in the Accelerated Dragon, apparently.
3.d4 cxd4 4.♘xd4 ♘c6 5.c4
This is the principled way of dealing with the Accelerated Dragon move

Anish Giri: 'In terms of the result, my win against the World Champion definitely stands out'

order. White is grabbing the opportunity to build a strong Maroczy Bind structure, defined by the e4- and c4-pawns, which tightly control the central light squares.
5...♘f6 6.♘c3 d6 7.♗e2 ♘xd4

A move order finesse preventing White from defending his knight with ♗e3.
8.♕xd4 ♗g7 9.0-0
The modern touch. The traditional way is to go ♗e3/♕d2, which appears healthier. But there are nuances.
9...0-0 10.♕d3 The queen stands a little oddly on d3, but the computers don't mind and neither did I.
10...a5 11.♗e3

11...♗d7!? This move surprised me a bit. I had expected Black to use the opportunity to grab space by pushing his a-pawn: 11...a4 12.♗d4 ♗d7 13.b4 axb3 14.axb3. This was the kind of position I didn't mind playing. Black is still short of space, and although he is happy to trade some pieces, the now isolated b-pawn may become weak.

12.♗d4
I decided to keep things very simple. More principled is keeping the dark-squared bishops on the board, although ...♗d7-c5 would descend on my queen with tempo.
12...♗c6 13.b3 ♘d7 14.♗xg7 ♔xg7 15.♕d4+ Embracing a potential ...♕b6 trade. **15...♔g8 16.♖fd1 ♕b6 17.♕xb6 ♘xb6 18.f4**

White is not playing for much here, but I still have more space, and the position seemed easy to play. Magnus, having pretty much solved his opening problems, decided that it was time to play for more, which to me felt quite premature at this point.
18...f5 An interesting decision, but it did him no good.
19.exf5 ♖xf5 20.g3 g5
Black is trying to trade my central pawns, but his pieces lack harmony, which I was able to exploit.

21.♗d3

I decided this was simple and strong, but I had missed an even more challenging continuation.

Here 21.♗g4! is even more accurate: 21...♖c5 22.♖e1! gxf4 23.♖xe7 fxg3 24.♖f1! (this seemed too far-fetched to me, but it actually works quite well) 24...gxh2+ 25.♔xh2 ♖g5 26.♗e6+ ♔h8 27.♖ff7 ♖h5+ 28.♔g3. White's rooks on the 7th rank dominate, the white king can run, while Black's is stuck in the corner, facing the unpleasant idea of ♘e2-f4.

21...♖c5 22.♖e1

22...♖e8
Natural. 22...gxf4! would lead to equality: 23.♖xe7 fxg3 24.hxg3 ♖h5. Here I liked the look of my position, but it seems Black has nothing to worry about, as 25.♘e4 is met solidly by 25...♖f8!, guarding against ♘f6+ and mobilizing his pieces.
23.♘e4! Trading a set of minor pieces and gaining momentum.
23...♗xe4 24.♖xe4 gxf4 25.♖xf4

All in all, Black can be happy with some of the developments: he has traded my central pawns and can potentially post a good knight on e5. At the same time, he is not quite

coordinated yet and may experience concrete issues with his weak h7-pawn and exposed king.
25...♘d7
Black needs to reroute this knight.
26.♖e1 ♘e5 27.♗e4
Tempo play, hitting the b7-pawn.

27...b5
Another good positional trade. Black now gets connected passed pawns in the centre, but the trade also costs him some of his piece coordination. 27...b6! would have avoided the issues Magnus is suddenly facing.
28.cxb5 ♖xb5 29.♖h4!
Asking Black a concrete question. After the natural 29...♘g6 there suddenly are some complications with 30.♗c6.

29...♖b4?!
A shocking decision; but I understood where Magnus was coming from. After the obvious 29...♘g6 Black may end up in a dangerous-looking bishop vs. knight endgame in which White will not have to take any difficult decisions of his own. This was a practical move in a way, but it certainly backfired.
As said, after 29...♘g6 the point

was 30.♗c6!: 30...♘xh4 31.♗xe8 (it's important to grab this rook first, as there is ... ♘d3!-♘c1! after the 31.♗xb5? ♘f3+ 32.♔f2 ♘xe1 33.♗xe8 sequence) 31...♘f3+ 32.♔f2 ♘xe1 (I also calculated 32...♘f5 here, when White has a strong intermezzo: 33.♗d7!, followed by 34.♖xe7, with a large advantage) 33.♗xb5 ♘c2

ANALYSIS DIAGRAM

I wouldn't know how to judge whether this endgame is fine for Black and if so, how comfortable it would be for him to play. All I could see is that White was having easy play, with passed pawns on both sides of the board, whereas Black's central pawns are still quite slow. The computers, however, are much better at judging such things these days, and point out that this endgame is objectively a draw.
30.♗xh7+ ♔g7 31.♗e4!
Better to return without allowing Black to neutralize my queenside pawn majority by allowing the a5-pawn to recapture on b4.

31...a4 Black has to start defending this pawn down endgame. I thought the idea might have been 31...♖xe4, which seemed interesting: going for

And there goes the king to g4. With little material left on the board, Anish Giri threatens mate and there is nothing Magnus Carlsen can do to stop it.

a rook ending with two connected central pawns vs my two sets of connected flank pawns. I assumed this was probably lost for Black, although it seemed so unusual that I wasn't completely sure.

After 31...♖xe4 32.♖hxe4 ♘f3+ 33.♔f2 ♘xe1 34.♔xe1 e5 35.♖a4 d5 36.♖xa5 d4 Black seems to be short a tempo. With White to move, this odd rook ending is winning. White can either push the b-pawn or try to prevent Black from activating his king by pushing g4, h4 instead.

32.bxa4 ♖xa4

33.♖e2 The most obvious human move, but the engine points out the sophisticated 33.♖h7+! ♔g8

34.♖h5!, ever so slightly improving the position of the rook and using the ♖xa2 ♗d5+ tactic. It is better to keep all four rooks on the board, since Black's king is in danger here.

33...♖h8

A good defensive attempt. Black is losing time and misplaces his king in the corner, but trading off a set of rooks is essential, otherwise ♖h7+ would always be in the air.

34.♖xh8 ♔xh8 35.♗d5!

A strong move. From here on in, my plan is to slowly advance my kingside pawns, while concentrating on trying to slow down Black's central pawns as much as possible. 35.♗d5! is a good first step, stopping ...e6.

35...♖a5?! Not the best. **36.♗b3 ♘c6** A good try, preparing ...e5 and ...♘d4, trying to get some counterplay.

37.♖d2!
Another strong move, stopping the ...e5, ...♘d4 idea. Now it became clear to me that I was winning. Black just doesn't have any counterplay.

37...♔g7 38.♔g2 ♘e5 39.h3
This is fine, intending g4, ♔g3, but 39.h4!, followed by ♔h3, would have been more energetic.

39...♘d7

40.♖e2! Another accurate move, preventing counterplay with ...♘c5.

40...♔f8 41.♖f2+ I played this stage of the game well. Now Black doesn't have a comfortable response.

41...♘f6 42.g4 White keeps advancing, while Black remains unable to create any play of his own.

42...♔g7 43.♖f4
Decent enough, and intending h4, amongst other things.

43...d5 44.g5?!
Better was the sophisticated 44.♖b4!, getting the rook out of the way and starting to annoy Black from the side.

44...♘e4

Luciano Pavarotti: 'How can you stay in front of an audience and say something if you don't believe in it. There is no bluff in this profession, it's not a poker game. It is a chess game. And if you lose, you don't have any excuse.' *(The legendary tenor on the art of opera)*

Santosh Hassan Sampath: 'This game is going on my CV for sure, and now that my bosses like me maybe I should ask for a good appraisal.' *(The Oracle financial controller and Indian amateur, who only 10 min before the start of the FIDE Online World Corporate Championship, discovered he was to play Magnus Carlsen)*

Annie Lord: 'We glugged the whole of *The Queen's Gambit* like a Fanta Orange.' *(The UK freelance writer, describing in the Guardian how she and her family lived vicariously during lockdown by binge-viewing the best TV)*

Theo Thijssen: 'On the other hand, chess did appeal to him. Chess was a swell game. Various famous chess players had gone crazy, that's the kind of a game it was.' *(From Dutch writer's 1923 classic, 'Kees the Boy')*

John Holland Rose: 'An intimate conversation without a word exchanged; a quivering activity in calm; triumph and defeat, hope and discouragement, life and death, all within the limit of 64 boxes: poetry and science reconciled: the ancient East with modern Europe – this is Chess.' *(The influential English historian (1855-1942) and biographer of William Pitt the Younger and French emperor Napoleon Bonaparte)*

Simon Williams: 'The beauty of chess is it can be whatever you want it to be. It transcends language, age, race, religion, politics, gender, and socioeconomic background. Whatever your circumstances, anyone can enjoy a good fight to the death over the chessboard.'

Vasily Smyslov: 'In the art of chess, there are no unalterable laws governing the struggle which are appropriate to every position, otherwise chess would lose its attractiveness and eternal character.' *(The seventh World Champion, who was born on 24 March, 1921, one hundred years ago)*

Eve Babitz: 'I was a naked pawn for art.' *(The artist and author in Esquire magazine in 1991, recalling her infamous Julien Wasser photo, when she played naked in a chess match in 1963 against Marcel Duchamp at the Pasadena Art Museum)*

Michael Stean: 'It was, I suppose, the cerebral version of landing a man on the moon. It was to prove the Soviet superiority over the Western systems that they could produce and control the World Chess Championship.' *(The English GM interviewed on the 19 March BBC World Service series 'Witness History', on the 1978 World Championship Match between Karpov and Kortchnoi, billed as 'the dirtiest chess match in history')*

Mikhail Tal: 'I have always thought it a matter of honour for every chess player to deserve the smile of fortune.'

Dominic Lawson: 'Just as the gun enables the inconsequential loner to somehow "equalise" himself with, say, John Lennon or John F. Kennedy, so the computer allows the talentless to prove themselves "better" than celebrated grandmasters.' *(From the former Sunday Telegraph editor and now president of the English Chess Federation, in his 1993 book The Inner Game)*

Ezra Pound: 'And the good writer chooses his words for their "meaning", but that meaning is not a set, cut-off thing like the move of knight or pawn on a chessboard. It comes up with roots, with associations, with how and where the world is familiarly used, or where it has been used brilliantly or memorably.' *(The American poet and critic, 1885-1972)*

"Manny": 'If you're a chess player and you haven't read this book ... I'm struggling to complete the sentence. It's sort of like you claim to be a Christian, but haven't read the Bible. You'd better do something about it!' *(The Good Read online reviewer on Bobby Fischer's timeless tome, My 60 Memorable Games)*

45.♗xd5?

A very poor decision. It's true that the position becomes even easier with a set of pawns gone – which was an argument in our time-trouble – but this still gives Black far more drawing chances than keeping both the connected passers.

After 45.h4 e6 the reply 46.♖g4! (intending h5) is very hard to find, however: 46...♔g6 47.♔f3 ♘d2+ 48.♔f4 ♘xb3 49.axb3, and White is dominating in this rook ending, with ♖g3 to follow.

45...♘xg5 46.♗b3

This is the start of new phase in the game. It is now clear that, without connected passers, Black has nothing to look forward to, but with so little material left, the drawing tendencies increase. If we imagine Black for example giving up his knight for the a2-pawn and trading the rooks, the game would be a draw.

46...e5? 46...♖e5! was a huge resource, crucially getting the knight back into the game via e4. We both missed it, however.

47.♖a4

Now White is objectively winning again. I offered a took trade, seeing

that the knight would be unable to sacrifice itself for the a-pawn.

47...♖c5 48.♖c4?!

Switching back and forth a little, but with the rook gone from c4, a far stronger option was to push h4 to prevent ...♘e6. Quite clumsy of me to allow it, although I'd have to say that time was a serious factor at this point.

48...♖a5?

A better defence would have been 48...♖b5!, preventing the ♖a4 switch.

49.h4?! Not the best moment to push this pawn, since it allows ...♘e6. Objectively, though, White is likely still winning.

But 49.♖g4! would have been the classiest solution: 49...♔h6 (after 49...♔f6 White wins by force: 50.♖a4 ♖c5 51.♖c4 ♖a5 52.h4!

ANALYSIS DIAGRAM

(now 52...♘e6 loses to 53.♖c6!, which is why 49.♖g4! had to be played first) 52...♘h7 53.♖c7!, and wins) 50.♖a4 ♖c5 51.h4 ♘h7 52.♖c4 ♖a5 53.♖c6+, and White has a good version of things, having gained a lot of tempi to push back Black's pieces and activate his own.

49...♘e6 50.♖a4 ♘f4+ I was

okay with this intermezzo, as I got to activate my king with tempo. But it would still have been better not to allow the knight to get to this decent and relatively centralized outpost.

51.♔f3 ♖c5 52.♖c4

The immediate 52.♔g4! is White's best option, according to the engine.

52...♖a5? The computer strongly prefers 52...♖b5! here, but in a human time-scramble you'd have to play it for intuitive reasons, not concrete ones. At this point, though, we had established the ♖a4-c4 and ...♖a5-c5 pattern, which we mostly used to gain time on the clock.

53.♖c7+ ♔h6 Objectively speaking, Black was lost here anyway, but now his king stumbles into a mating net.

54.♗c2!

I suspect Magnus had seen this and thought that he could defend with ...♖a3+ and ...♘d3. Unfortunately for him, however, this is still losing.

54...♖a3+ 55.♔g4 ♘d3

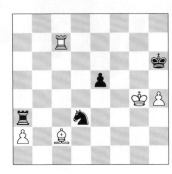

56.♔f5! The only winning move. I was quite pleased to have found this in my final seconds.

56...♘b4 56...e4 would probably have been the best practical try, when

White would have had to find one more strong sequence: 57.♔xe4 ♘b4

ANALYSIS DIAGRAM

and here the only winning move is 58.♔e5!, when after 58...♔h5 59.♖h7+ ♔g4 60.♗f5+ ♔g3 61.♔f6! (accurate) 61...♖xa2 62.h5 ♔f4 63.♖d7 the h-pawn is unstoppable. Not an easy sequence to find.

57.♗e4! Now the knight on b4 is clearly dominated. Black is already lost, but with his next move Magnus allows for a picturesque finale.

57...♖xa2

57...♘d3 would have prolonged the game, but the rook ending is winning: 58.♗xd3 ♖xd3 59.♔xe5 ♖a3 60.♖c2 ♔h5 61.♖h2. This would have been the easiest, keeping the pawn and intending to transfer the king to the queenside, although some work would still need to be done.

I had once seen a study like this. These flank-pawn positions can get quite complicated.

58.♔g4!

A beautiful position. With so little material on the board, the mate with ♖h7+ is completely unstoppable. A study-like finish.

■ ■ ■

'Nepo' only managed a single draw after his opening victory, which created an easy diagnosis of 'distracted by looming resumption of the Candidates'. Ian's troubles included a lovely piece of work from Tata Steel winner Jorden van Foreest, who produced a game of classical calibre.

NOTES BY
Jorden van Foreest

Jorden van Foreest
Ian Nepomniachtchi
Magnus Carlsen Invitational
2021 (prelim 5)
Modern Defence

At this point I had 1 point out of 4 games and I was not quite pleased. Therefore I decided to go all in in this game. Quite a reckless decision, which easily could've turned out badly. I just really wanted to end the day on a good note.
1.e4 g6 2.d4 ♗g7 3.♘f3 d6 4.♗e3

A clever idea, which has recently become quite popular. The reason for postponing the development of the knight will soon become clear.
4...a6 5.c4!?
This reveals the main point of the line. All of a sudden we have a typical KID position where the move ...a6 usually is not very useful.
5...♘c6 6.h3 e5 7.d5 ♘ce7 8.♘c3 f5 9.g4!?

A bold move that makes the position very sharp. I was thinking that since I am ahead in development I should try and open up the position.
9...♘f6 10.gxf5 gxf5 11.♖g1

With the rook occupying the g-file I thought there should be good attacking chances.
11...0-0 12.♗d3 ♔h8 13.♕c2 f4 14.♗d2 c6 15.0-0-0 b5!
Black has fended off my attack for the time being and is opening up the position on the other side of the board. Up to this point I had been playing very fast and I started wondering exactly what kind of mess I had gotten myself into. However, before I could worry too much I noticed a strong move which made me quite optimistic.

16.c5! A strike in the centre which I was quite happy to find. While keeping lanes closed on the queenside for the moment, I am attempting to open up the position for my own pieces to attack the opponent's king.
16...b4 17.♘a4 cxd5 18.exd5 ♘exd5 19.♘g5 ♗d7 20.♗c4!
An important resource, freeing the way for the queen along the b1-h7 diagonal. Suddenly Black has to worry about all kinds of mating threats.

Celeb 64
John Henderson

Mick Schumacher

The 2021 Formula 1 season started in late March with the Bahrain Grand Prix and an epic dogfight between Lewis Hamilton's Mercedes and Max Verstappen's Red Bull. Also in the spotlight of the petrol-heads was the debut performance of rookie driver Mick Schumacher, the youngest son of the 7-time world champion Michael. Coming up through the ranks with an iconic surname in the global sport, expectations were sky-high for the new 22-year-old Haas driver who won last year's F2 title. And so Schumacher junior relaxed before his big day with his favourite pastime: chess! When he got on the track, though, he found it tough going on his debut. He spun off in the early stages and finished 16th. Certainly an inauspicious start to his F1 career, but like his father, Mick is a long-term strategic thinker, who admits that he hones that skill playing chess. In the paddock, he prefers to exercise his mind and memory, devising strategies while learning to anticipate an opponent's next move, as he immerses himself in the game.
Yet despite living in the fast lane, it's already been noted by the media that while his rivals are riveted to their phones or computers off the track, there's no such digital activity from Schumacher junior. He prefers to keep it all old school and tactile with a wooden chess set and board, as he takes on members of his pit crew and entourage. ∎

20...♖c8! Of course, Nepo doesn't wait for my attack and creates threats of his own. **21.♗xd5**

21...♗xa4?
An unfortunate blunder in a highly complex position. Black cannot afford to give up his bishop as it was not only a key attacker, but also an important defender for his own king. Instead, the strong 21...♕a5! would have put the ball back in my court.
In fact, I had seen 21...♕a5 and I was not sure how to respond to it as Black's threats seemed stronger than my own. However, 22.♘e6 ♗xa4 23.♗b3! seems to be a strong continuation, combining attack and defence. The position should be in a dynamic equilibrium.
22.♕xa4 ♘xd5

After a hesitant start in his Tour debut, Tata Steel winner Jorden van Foreest doggedly fought back to win a couple of good games.

23.♔b1? Honestly speaking, I do not know why I didn't just go for the fork with 23.♘e6. I could not see a refutation but felt there may be something. As it turns out Black has nothing and White would have been winning.
23...♕f6? This felt natural to me, but in fact it is a mistake. Nepo must have missed my trick on move 27. Better would have been 23...♕e7, putting Black firmly back in the game.
24.♕c2!

This sudden return of the white queen, threatening mate in one, forces Black to parry with a rather awkward queen move himself.
24...♕h6 25.c6 ♘e7

For now it seems that Black rounds up the dangerous c6-pawn and he should be doing fine.
26.♗xb4 ♖xc6 27.♖xd6!
Quite an attractive shot, if I may say so myself. All the tactics work like clockwork and Black is forced to seek chances in a desperate endgame.
27...♖xc2 28.♖xh6 ♗xh6 29.♔xc2

Material is equal, but Black is in terrible shape. Both the nasty pin on the knight and the ongoing mating threats are hard to deal with.
29...♖c8+ 30.♔d3 ♖d8+ 31.♔e2 ♗xg5 32.♖xg5 ♘g6 Black seems to have survived, and given a couple moves to consolidate his position he would be fine. However, with every next move White creates a threat that ultimately makes Black lose a vital pawn. **33.♗c3 ♔g8**

34.h4! 34.♗xe5 would be ill-advised, since after 34...♖e8 it is suddenly Black who wins.
34...♔f7 35.♖h5! ♔e6
Black decides to give up on one of the pawns for some activity. 35...♖h8 hangs on to the pawn for the moment, but after 36.♔f3 and 37.♔e4, Black loses material and the game anyway.

**36.♖xh7 e4 37.♖h6 ♚f5 38.♖h5+
♚e6 39.♖h6 ♚f5 40.♖h5+ ♚e6**

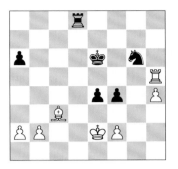

41.♖g5! A final accurate touch that stops any counterplay by Black.
**41...♘xh4 42.♖e5+ ♚f7 43.♖xe4
♘g6 44.♚f3**

White is a healthy pawn to the good while the bishop is far superior to the knight. The rest is a matter of (not too difficult) technique.
**44...♖d6 45.♖c4 ♚e6 46.♚e4
♖b6 47.♗d4 ♖d6 48.♖c7 ♘h4
49.b4 ♘f5 50.♗c5 ♖d2 51.♖c6+
♚d7 52.♖xa6 ♘h4 53.♚xf4
♘g2+ 54.♚e4 ♘e1 55.b5 ♖b2
56.♖a7+ ♚c8 57.a4**

And Black resigned.

■ ■ ■

The contours of the knock-out field started to come into focus in the course of the second session of the Preliminaries. Anish Giri began with two wins to create an impressive five-in-a row streak, and ended with 8/10 after finishing his day with Mamedyarov's scalp. Magnus matched Giri's hot pace, and was still just half a point behind after Day 2. With Carlsen's lack of tour victories the repetitive headline story, it was easy to forget that he had won all of the Preliminaries.

Wesley So shifted gears dramatically and moved into very safe territory. The other early tour titan, the habitually unbeatable Teimour Radjabov, dropped below 50% after a pair of shock defeats. Aronian had a disastrous session, and looked set to lose his fourth game of the day before Jorden van Foreest blundered into mate.

The end of the Preliminaries tends to be a stark contrast between the dull requirements of those in possession of safe KO spots, and the heroics of those who rise up and grab them. Ian Nepomniachtchi was the sparkler, going completely turbo and taking 4/5 to qualify comfortably, also handing Giri his only defeat. This was enough to give the World Champion yet another Preliminary first.

Levon Aronian took the final playoff berth, a +1 finish just enough to eliminate Sergey Karjakin on tiebreak. Fan favourite Daniil Dubov also fell just short with the only 50% score, and there was no comeback from Radjabov.

Teenager Alireza Firouzja made his first advance from the prelims for this tour, and he was in fact the only new KO face in this event.

You would expect qualification drama to be in focus, but in fact, one of the short draws between frontrunners captured much of the attention in the final round... There was the excitement that Magnus Carlsen and Hikaru Nakamura produced with their remarkable opening choice.

The Double Bongcloud: Double question marks??

A heated discussion erupted when Magnus Carlsen and Hikaru Nakamura went for a quick draw in the last round of the Preliminaries. Not because they made a draw (at least not in the first place), but mainly because of how they did it.

This is a game that wouldn't have been possible without the online boom fanned by a year of lockdown, stars streaming video, and maybe even a hit Netflix series. What follows is one of the aspects of fame for the game, but also quite a bit more.

**Magnus Carlsen
Hikaru Nakamura**
Magnus Carlsen Invitational
2021 (prelim 15)
1.e4 e5 2.♔e2

This is the now infamous Bongcloud opening, which came to the shocked attention of the mainstream chess world after Hikaru Nakamura played it vs. Jeffery Xiong in the St. Louis online blitz last year. I quizzed Magnus about the Bongcloud after St. Louis, and his basic verdict was that it was just a move – and you either tried to punish it, or returned the favour.

A bit of research will show it that it is a popular... occurrence in online streaming of high-speed games. Historians may be interested to know that the name is not a reference to the state of mind associated with this kind of opening, but apparently refers to a legendary online player. ▶

In a Chess.com forum conversation begun in early 2008, the roots of the opening are explored in 'the life and times' of user Lenny.Bongcloud, who espoused a chess philosophy involving king marches. There were – are? – apparently a host of variants, from the original King (Lenny Bongcloud: Get your King to the opposite back rank to win), to the Cinderella, Hobbit and many other Bongclouds.

My favourite is the 'Honeymoon', where King and Queen must make the trip together, 'for luv, dued', according to Lenny. Lenny's dedication apparently earned the second-lowest rating on the server.

2...♚e7

The Double BongCloud?
3.♔e1 ♚e8 4.♔e2 ♚e7 5.♔e1 ♚e8 6.♔e2 ♚e7 ½-½.

In separate interviews, maverick Magnus and tournament winner Anish shared their thoughts with me about the occasion and the opening. To begin with, what was Magnus's thought process when deciding to play the Bongcloud and what was he expecting to happen? There was still something at stake, even though he and Hikaru had both qualified.

Magnus Carlsen: 'It was definitely a gamble, but it was a calculated gamble – I was *pretty* sure that he would return the favour just for, you know, the memes or whatever. I was at least 90% sure that Maxime and Anish would make a draw and that a draw would secure me the first seed, so exactly what I thought was going to happen, happened.

Magnus Carlsen: 'It was definitely a gamble, but it was a calculated gamble'

'Also, I don't think playing something normal there was what his fans would have wanted. I was pretty sure it would have been the same as playing some other actual drawish line.'

So, what did Anish make of the Bongcloud draw incident?

Anish Giri: 'I see it as a move that has the disadvantage of losing king safety and all that, but it has the advantage of putting pressure on your opponent. It puts *ginormous* pressure and takes it away from you.

'If you lose you can say – of course, what do you expect? If you don't lose, though, you gain – so much. It will haunt the other guy, or at least it could, especially in the case of Hikaru.

'So I see ♔e2 as a move with psychological advantages. And I see a response to that, with ...♚e7, as a move that sacrifices your advantage on the board, but gives back that psychological thing.'

Of course, shock was expressed by the traditionally minded sector, one notable being former FIDE bigwig Ali Nihat Yazici trumpeting his displeasure on Twitter. He wondered what was the greatest scandal: a short draw, the Bongcloud, or FIDE's silence on the matter.

Magnus Carlsen: 'Most of the reactions were sort of external – some grievances from colleagues, especially people who don't have much work at all these days. To see the top players deliberately tossing games in that manner, I can understand why that would be infuriating.

'But I think you have to see these things in context: If I'm going to play 15 games in the Preliminaries, usually at least 11 of them will be real tough

fighting games, so one sort of dead rubber last-round game...

'It got the tournament extra attention. That's not what it's all about, but I don't think it's necessarily a bad thing. In general, it's way too much of a gamble to be profitable, but in this case it was the perfect opponent and the perfect set of circumstances.

'Using this as an example for why online chess is bad and why I don't respect the game and so on is obviously a huge oversimplification at best.'

Anish Giri: 'I don't see how it could be offensive to someone. I definitely don't see it as a sign of disrespect. For me chess is a game that you try to win. It runs so deep in me that I can't understand or imagine that it could be different for any of my competitors. So I look at this move from the viewpoint of someone who is trying to win.

'Not only win the game today, perhaps, but also leave a mark for future battles. I see the point of ♔e2. I also see the downsides – that there are people who will be online harassing you for a while. That's also part of it.

'On the other hand, I wouldn't want to do this. I'm probably not very good at playing these kind of positions (laughs). I don't like an unsafe king and I don't like disharmony, so I would probably lose this game and I would be upset. And that small chance that I wouldn't lose, I wouldn't really feel that much joy that I had humiliated my opponent or anything.

'I played a Bongcloud online once against Indian comedians, they made me play it, because they said it is like a handicap.

'I'm surprised Magnus took this decision and I understand Hikaru's motives as well. Hikaru had so much to lose. I think overall, as long as nobody gets harassed, I don't think these two got harassed personally, any fuss around chess is good.

'I was quite interested in why they did it and I guess I understand it. And, in a way it served the purpose of "hashtag: growing the game".' ∎

Cold shower for Firouzja

Pre-tournament favourites Carlsen and So were majestic in their quarter-final matches. Magnus seized the lead on both days, and never needed a fourth game to eliminate Aronian. Wesley gave the sensational Firouzja a stark demonstration of the level needed here, winning 2½-½ both days. The game that set the pace on day two was particularly memorable.

NOTES BY
Wesley So

Wesley So
Alireza Firouzja
Magnus Carlsen Invitational
2021 (qf 2.2)
Caro-Kann, Advance Variation

1.e4 I decided to stick to my main first move 1.e4, which has worked well in the past. **1...c6** After having not much success with the Sicilian in the first game the previous day, Alireza switched to his favourite opening, the Caro-Kann Defence. It's the opening he used to great effect last year in Stavanger, Norway. Being in a must-win situation (Firouzja was two games down -ed.), the Caro-Kann allows Black resources to complicate the game and muddy the waters.
Our Sicilian game had gone as follows: 1...c5 2.♘f3 d6 3.♗b5+ ♗d7 4.♗xd7+ ♕xd7 5.c4 ♘f6 6.♘c3 g6 7.d4 cxd4 8.♘xd4 ♗g7 9.f3 ♕c7 10.b3 ♕a5 11.♗d2 ♘c6 12.♘de2 0-0 13.0-0 ♘d7 14.♔h1 ♘c5 15.♘d5 ♕d8 16.♗c3 ♗xc3 17.♘dxc3 a6 18.a4 ♖c8 19.♖b1

ANALYSIS DIAGRAM

and Black had a depressing position.
2.d4 d5 3.e5

After thinking for some time I decided to stay true to the Advance Variation, as this has given me good results in the past. I've also worked quite a bit on this variation beforehand, so I was ready to go all out with it. Although 3.e5 is the most principled continuation against the Caro-Kann, it is also the most complex, as it keeps all the pieces on the board.
3... ♗f5 4.♘f3
I've also played 4.♘d2 in the past, and it can transpose to similar variations as in the game.
4...e6 5.♗e2 ♘e7 5...c5 is the main line here, but Alireza prefers to keep more pieces on the board.
6.0-0

6...h6
Black takes control of the g5-square and frees up h7 for his bishop. This variation is very dynamic, as he creates an initiative on the kingside. Alireza had played these lines a few times before and I knew that when making my preparation.
His other favourite move here is 6...

c5, immediately fighting for control of the centre.
7.♘bd2
This is the main reply, developing the queenside knight. Hundreds of games have been played here.
The day before I played 7.a4, gaining space on the queenside, but it was probably too ambitious as Black got counterplay on the other flank: 7...g5 8.a5 a6 9.b4 ♘d7 10.c3 f6! 11.exf6 ♘g6 12.f7+ ♔xf7 13.♘bd2 ♗d6 14.♘b3 ♕c7 15.g3 ♘f6 16.♗d3 g4 17.♘e1 h5

ANALYSIS DIAGRAM

and Black had a large advantage, although later I was able to defend tenaciously, So-Firouzja, 3rd game of the quarter final, ½-½, 66).
7...♘d7 8.♘b3 g5 9.♗d2
This is the best place for the dark-squared bishop, where it controls a5 and b4.
9...a5
Fighting for space on the queenside. Black can also play 9...♕c7 first, followed by ...a5 next move.
10.a4 ♕c7

11.c3 This is quite a rare move and the idea is to keep solid control over the centre. It has been played in a few

NEW FRITZTRAINER DVDs

Let Jan Werle show you how to beat the King's Indian and Benoni structures with the Saemisch Variation!

Improve your handling of the bishop by means of Merijn van Delft's interactive training course.

Or let Sipke Ernst provide you with a great arsenal of fresh ideas in the Open Spanish!

JAN WERLE:
THE SAEMISCH VARIATION AGAINST THE KING'S INDIAN AND BENONI

Beat the King's Indian and Benoni structures with the impenetrable pawn phalanx g2-f3-e4-d5. Encounter your opponent with sound and fresh ideas in this classical rebooted line of the Saemisch! The centre is stabilised with the move f3, and a possible expansion on the kingside is also prepared. Thus it is usually White who gets the attacking chances against the king. Since Benoni is structurally very similar to the King's Indian with ...c5, many plans and motifs can be transferred here. You can then test both your theoretical knowledge as well as look at typical ideas in model games in the numerous accompanying interactive videos. Video running time: more than 7 hours (English). With interactive training including video feedback, database with model games and more!

29,90 €

MERIJN VAN DELFT:
PRACTICAL CHESS STRATEGY: THE BISHOP

When it comes to strategy, one of the key things that chess professionals understand much better than amateur players is the role of the bishop. Why do two bishops ("the bishop pair") complement each other to such an extent that they are a major long term force? How is being a long-range piece an essential trademark of the bishop? Why do strong players regularly tuck their bishop away on its initial square? Questions like these will be examined on this strategy video course. One of the most persistent misunderstandings among chess fans is that positions with opposite-coloured bishops are drawish. In fact, opposite-coloured bishops tend to make the position sharper and are a favourite and often

winning weapon of World Champion Magnus Carlsen. The way the bishop moves is much easier to grasp for beginners than the way the knight moves, but, paradoxically, its ways turn out to be more mysterious. Sometimes a seemingly bad bishop turns out to be a good bishop. Experienced trainer IM Merijn van Delft from the Netherlands has carefully selected 12 instructive games. The games are thoroughly analysed and played through with the interactive Chessbase video software. Every one of these games will provide you with a serious training session. Good luck and enjoy!

29,90 €

SIPKE ERNST:
THE FLEXIBLE OPEN SPANISH

The Open Spanish (.e4 e5 2.Nf3 Nc6 3.Bb5 a6 4.Ba4 Nf6 5.0-0 Nxe4) is considered to be one of the soundest systems in modern opening theory. It remains a popular choice among superstars such as Mamedyarov, Caruana , So and Giri and was used in World Championship matches by Korchnoi and Anand. In this opening Black opts for active piece play and is not afraid to fight for the initiative from an early stage. One of the many good features of this opening is that Black is often the side which controls the pace of the game. Black can go for long forced variations that lead to sharp endgames or choose a slower game with more pieces on the board. Therefore, the Open Spanish is not only an excellent weapon against stronger players but also gives plenty of scope for the outplaying of "lesser rated" opponents. This DVD offers a full repertoire for Black against 1.e4 e5 2.Nf3 Nc6 3.Bb5 and gives you a great arsenal of ideas against all the topical lines. Video running time: 4 hours . With interactive training including video feedback, database with model games and more!

29,90 €

ChessBase GmbH · News: en.chessbase.com · CB Shop: shop.chessbase.com
CHESSBASE DEALER: NEW IN CHESS · P.O. Box 1093 · NL-1810 KB Alkmaar
phone (+31)72 5127137 · fax (+31)72 5158234 · WWW.NEWINCHESS.COM

email games recently and it seems like a strong move.

The main line here is 11.♖c1, protecting the c2-pawn and preparing c4. I've played this move before in the past and it's also a decent choice.

The immediate 11.♘e1 prepares f4 but allows 11...c5, when after 12.c3 c4 13.♘c1 f6 Black is able to get good counterplay in the centre.

11...f6 Black came to this game well prepared. This is the best choice for him at this point.

The point of c3 is that after 11...♗g7 White goes 12.♘e1 followed by f4, when the bishop on g7 is blockaded by my solid centre pawns.

11...♗g6 has been played in a few games in my database. They continued with 12.c4 ♗g7 13.♖c1 0-0 14.cxd5 ♘xd5 15.h4 g4 16.♘e1 h5 17.♗d3 and White is slightly better thanks to the space advantage and the passive bishop on g7.

11...c5 fails to impress with the knight still on f3: 12.dxc5 ♗g7 13.♗b5 and White is better.

12.exf6 ♘g6

13.c4 The move 13.♘e5 is also interesting at this point. White sacrifices

a pawn for the initiative: 13...♘dxe5 14.dxe5 ♕xe5 15.♗h5. I believe this position is quite difficult to defend for Black.

13...♗d6
Following the critical variation.
13...♘xf6 14.♘e5 is good for White as g4 is a threat and Black loses control over the e5-square.
Here I spent some time trying to remember my analysis, as at this point White is at a crucial juncture.

14.cxd5
This has a very concrete follow-up. The main alternative is 14.f7+ ♔xf7 15.g3. Black's king is quite vulnerable on f7, and I think White has a small

and risk-free advantage. 15...g4 leads nowhere due to 16.♘e1 and after his best 15...♖hf8 16.♗c3 ♔g8 17.c5 ♗e7 18.♘e1 e5 19.♘g2 White has a small but stable advantage.
14.c5 also looks attractive but after 14...♗f4 15.g3 ♗xd2 16.♘fxd2 ♘xf6! it turns out that Black can just sacrifice a piece: 17.g4 ♗e4 18.f3 h5! 19.fxe4 hxg4 20.e5 ♕h7 21.♖f2 g3 and Black's counterplay is enough for equality.

14...exd5

15.♗d3!
A brilliant and important move. I knew this move was working well for White, but I couldn't exactly

remember all my analysis at this stage. The lines become very forcing. White gets a very powerful initiative in return for the piece, using the weakness of Black's king.

After the mundane 15.♕e1 0-0 16.♗xa5 b6 17.♗b4 ♖ae8 White has to be careful despite being up in material. Black's activity is quite threatening.

Just to mention, taking on a5 first does not work: 15.♗xa5 ♖xa5 16.♗d3 ♗e4!, closing down the e-file.

15...♗xd3 Black is obviously forced to go for the complications.

16.♗xa5 ♖xa5 17.♕xd3

17...♔f7! So far so good. Black has to move his king away from the e-file. It is quite clear to see that 17...♘f4 does not work well: 18.♖fe1+ (White has to give a check first, as after 18.♕f5 0-0 Black is able to castle and harass my queen) 18...♔f7 (18...♔d8 19.♕f5 ♖a8 and here both 20.f7 and 20.g3 are good for White, with more than enough compensation for the piece) 19.♕f5 ♖aa8

ANALYSIS DIAGRAM

and now 20.g3, kicking away the black knight. He can retreat with

He must have had high hopes after his splendid performance in Wijk aan Zee, but Alireza Firouzja had a rude awakening in the quarter-final clash with Wesley So.

20...♘g6 21.♕e6+ ♔f8 but here White has two pawns and more than enough compensation for the piece.

18.♘xa5

18...♕xa5?
This is a bad mistake, after which his position becomes very difficult.

Black had to counterattack on my knight with 18...g4! 19.♘e5+ ♘dxe5 20.dxe5 ♗xe5 and he is attacking both h2 and the knight on a5. White

has no more than a small advantage after 21.♘b3 ♗xh2+ 22.♔h1 ♕e5! (threatening ...♕h5 and mate) 23.♘d4 ♕h5 24.♕f5 ♕xf5 25.♘xf5 ♗e5. Black gets a pawn for the exchange, and thanks to his solid structure he has good chances to hold. This line is truly forcing, starting on move 18.

19.♕f5!

Black cannot take on f6 because of

Wesley So gave the sensational Firouzja a stark demonstration of the level needed here, winning 2½-½ both days

♘e5+. Now White should be winning by force thanks to the threat of ♖ae1.

19...♕d8 20.♖ae1

Threatening the mighty ♖e7+. I could have used the other rook as well to bring it to e1. Black has no defence.

20...♘gf8

20...♘xf6 21.♘e5+ wins material. And 20...♘df8 21.♖e7+! ♗xe7 22.fxe7+ ♔xe7 23.♖e1+ ♔d6 24.♘e5 wins for White as well, thanks to the threats of ♘f7+ and ♘xg6.

21.♖e7+! ♗xe7

22.fxe7+

In addition White has another win here with 22.♘xg5+! hxg5 23.fxe7+ ♔xe7 24.♕xg5+ and since ...♔e8 loses to ♖e1+ he has to go 24...♘f6 25.♕g7+. White grabs the rook on h8 and has a winning position, thanks to the three connected kingside pawns.

22...♔xe7 23.♖e1+

The immediate 23.♘e5 does not work well because of 23...♕a5, when Black is able to defend against the threats.

23...♔d6 24.♘e5

I spent some time earlier making sure that Black has no tricks left. ♘f7+ with a family fork is coming next move.

24...♖h7 24...♕a5 fails thanks to the fancy 25.♘c4+, forking the queen and the king. **25.♘xd7** A nice move to make. Black cannot take my knight on d7 in three different ways.

25...♕xd7 25...♖e7 does not really prolong the game since the king and pawn endgame is easily won after 26.♖xe7 ♕xe7 27.♕xf8 ♔xd7 28.♕xe7+ ♔xe7 29.g4, when Black is a pawn down.

26.♕e5 Mate.

A nice way to finish the game.

This match went very well. The same cannot be said concerning my last two matches with Anish Giri and Magnus Carlsen. I started running into problems and wasn't really able to get anything going in those. Perhaps playing four or five games everyday for nine days in a row took its toll. I'd like to give a big shoutout to Anish Giri for winning the major tournament.

■ ■ ■

The matches featuring the practising Candidates were far more dramatic. Times have changed since the regular final duels between Hikaru Nakamura and Magnus Carlsen on the inaugural tour. The crucible of gruelling events is forging a new set of specialists. The first day of the Nepo-Naka showdown was split, with the pair trading white wins and ending 2-2. On Day 2, the Russian was supreme, cruising to a 2-0 lead

Giri's pleasure in consistently playing both sides of sharp Sicilians was intriguing

and then fending off a last bit of determination from the American.

A close examination of the duel between Candidates Maxime Vachier-Lagrave and Anish Giri should provide pundits with plenty of speculative fuel about possible preparation and chances for that looming event. Giri's pleasure in consistently playing both sides of sharp Sicilians throughout the Magnus Invitational was intriguing, as was his success.

On Day 1, the rivals traded Black wins, but Maxime crashed out after his defences were breached on Day 2, losing both blacks, having finally resorted to a rickety Modern Defence for his last stand.

MC Invitational 2021(prelims)		elo rapid		TPR
1	Carlsen	NOR 2881	10½	2867
2	Giri	NED 2731	10	2845
3	So	USA 2741	9½	2822
4	Nakamura	USA 2829	9	2793
5	Nepomniachtchi	RUS 2778	8½	2768
6	Firouzja	FID 2703	8½	2773
7	Vachier-Lagrave	FRA 2860	8½	2762
8	Aronian	ARM 2778	8	2746
9	Karjakin	RUS 2709	8	2750
10	Dubov	RUS 2770	7½	2728
11	Radjabov	AZE 2758	7	2711
12	Mamedyarov	AZE 2761	6½	2689
13	Grandelius	SWE 2632	6	2669
14	Van Foreest	NED 2543	6	2675
15	Anton	ESP 2674	4	2564
16	Pichot	ARG 2548	2½	2475

Battles of nerves

The seeded pairings pitted the Tour favourites against the title cycle Candidates in the semi-finals: Carlsen-Nepomniachtchi and So-Giri. Magnus had made no secret about wanting a victory here over current tour leader Wesley So. Wesley won both of their final clashes this season, creating the spectre of a very different new decade by winning the first Tour final, the Skilling Open, on Magnus's 30th birthday last November. Magnus has yet to win an event since exiting his 20s.

At event's end, Magnus would both get his wish and rue the timing of his 'bad few days'. Nepo took the first set 2½-1½ after a sharp performance against a suddenly slightly wobbly Carlsen. This game would have a subtle echo in the final outcome of the entire event.

Magnus Carlsen
Ian Nepomniachtchi
Magnus Carlsen Invitational
2021 (sf 1.3)

position after 26.♗c3

White's last move, 26.♗d2-c3?, not only allows wily Ian a chance to land a sucker punch, it would also resonate and affect a pivotal decision in the event. Giri referenced this moment as an ingredient in the complex equation that convinced him to sacrifice a piece against Nepo in the first blitz game of their tiebreak in the Final.

26...♘f4!
Not a decisive blow, but the beginning of the table-turning.

27.gxf4! The best move, and one that impresses this old human. I can't help feeling that a more natural mortal reaction would be something like 27.♕d1 ♘xg2 28.♕xb3 cxb3 29.♘xg2

ANALYSIS DIAGRAM

after receiving a kingside related shock, but this is passive and grim, with Black having access to so many tasty outposts – the bishop will settle on e4 and the knight is set to torment the ♗c3.

27...♖g4 28.h3 ♖xh4 29.♗xb7 ♔xb7 30.♕f3+ ♔a6
At the very genuine risk of both sounding idiotic and insulting the World Champion, I have a kind of bizarre affection for Magnus's next move, even though it is a serious error. The idea of seeking counterplay by meeting ...♘d5 with the exchange sacrifice ♖xe6 is inherent in the position, and White decides to force this situation, while creating some space for the ♗c3. This has a definite element of the logical harmony that often powers the champ. But sometimes it is just reflexes – White's time deficit here was a fatal handicap.

31.d5?

31.a4 looks like real counterplay, trying to muss up the Black king's hair and hoping for the sacrifice later.
31...♘xd5 32.♖xe6 ♖xe6 33.♕xd5 ♖g6+ 34.♔f1 ♕b5

White has no sensible way to keep the queens on the board for long, and there are no technical obstacles to combat the material deficit.
35.♖d1 ♕xd5 36.♖xd5 ♖xf4 37.♗d4 ♖f3 38.♗e3 f4 39.♖f5 ♖e6 40.♗d4 ♖e4 41.♔g2 ♖d3 42.♗c3 d5 43.♖f6+ ♔b5 44.♖f7 d4 45.♗b4 ♖e2 0-1.

COLOPHON

PUBLISHER: Allard Hoogland
EDITOR-IN-CHIEF:
Dirk Jan ten Geuzendam
HONORARY EDITOR: Jan Timman
CONTRIBUTING EDITOR: Anish Giri
EDITORS: Peter Boel, René Olthof
PRODUCTION: Joop de Groot
TRANSLATOR: Piet Verhagen
SALES AND ADVERTISING: Remmelt Otten

PHOTOS AND ILLUSTRATIONS IN THIS ISSUE:
Alisa Studio, National Dutch Photo Archives, Max Euwe Centre, Maria Emelianova, Bard Gudim, Hines Collection, Jurriaan Hoefsmit/Tata Steel, Andreas Kontokanis, Eteri Kublashvili, Rob Mieremet, Collection Bruce Monson, Lennart Ootes, Berend Vonk

COVER PHOTO: New In Chess

COVER DESIGN: Hélène Bergmans

© No part of this magazine may be reproduced, stored in a retrieval system or transmitted in any form or by any means, recording or otherwise, without the prior permission of the publisher.

NEW IN CHESS
P.O. BOX 1093
1810 KB ALKMAAR
THE NETHERLANDS

PHONE: 00-31-(0)72-51 27 137
SUBSCRIPTIONS: nic@newinchess.com
EDITORS: editors@newinchess.com
ADVERTISING: otten@newinchess.com

WWW.NEWINCHESS.COM

The other Tour specialist also suffered a rude awakening, at the hands of 2021's man in form. Wesley So won the first game of their match with black, but Anish Giri struck back with a dramatic repeat of that opening in Game 3, then took the set with a determined black win of his own to end the day.

NOTES BY
Anish Giri

Anish Giri
Wesley So
Magnus Carlsen Invitational
2021 (sf 1.3)
Ruy Lopez, Berlin Defence

My semi-final match against Wesley So saw quite a few unforced errors and odd decisions from both sides. This game, too, is far from perfect, but it was an important one. After my loss on the first day and a quick draw in Game 2, little suggested that I would end up winning both mini-matches. This was the third game of the first day.
1.e4 e5 2.♘f3 ♘c6 3.♗b5 ♘f6
4.d3 ♗c5 5.♗xc6 dxc6 6.0-0

I played this system against Wesley in Game 1 as well. I handled the opening/early middlegame better than my opponent and got a large advantage, before ruining everything later on. But although I lost that, I had no reason not to continue with the same opening variation.
6...♘d7 7.c3 a5!?

Wesley decided to try and confuse me by postponing kingside castling. I should mention that Ding Liren also tried to be clever here, going for 7...h6!? to prevent ♗g5.
8.d4 ♗d6 9.♖e1
I decided to postpone the ♗g5 idea for now.
9...a4!?

Wesley keeps playing very inventively and delays castling once again.
10.♘bd2 exd4 11.cxd4 ♘b6!?
Another move before castling. This time, Black prevents ♘c4.
12.♘f1 0-0

13.♗g5?!
A practical decision, although I disliked it immediately.
If not for the match situation, I would probably have gone for the safer option: 13.♘g3 ♗g4, and here I didn't rate my winning chances after the inevitable trades very highly: 14.h3 ♗xf3 15.♕xf3 ♗xg3 16.♕xg3 ♕xd4, when the position felt too simplified for a must-win game.
13...f6 14.♗h4 ♗g4!
The bishop is rather annoying here, and it was clear to me now that the only way was pushing g4, which

would weaken my position considerably, given that my centre is not entirely stable.
15.h3 ♗h5 16.♕d3
Postponing g4 for one more move, although it is clear that it will have to come.
16...♕d7 17.g4
The only way to play ambitiously, even though I felt too overextended at this point.
17...♗g6

18.♘e3?!
A mistake, objectively speaking, but it was too late to try and play it safe anyway.
18.♗g3! would still have been better.
18...♘d5?!
Tempting, but actually it should have been prepared first. Now I am getting back into the game somewhat.
18...a3! would have been even more clever: 19.b3 ♗b4!, forcing the rook to misplace itself first. 20.♖e2 ♘d5!. Now this is a huge blow, with ...♘f4 and ...♘c3 coming.
19.♘f5!

Blocking the strong g6-bishop.
19...♘f4 The knight is annoying, but tolerably so.

20.♕f1 Ugly, but it does hold my position together. Here I started feeling slightly better about my position. Not that it's good now, but my centre is not collapsing just yet and there is some potential.

20...♗xf5 21.gxf5 g6
A good simplifying sequence.

22.♗g3! Threatening e5 and maintaining the intrigue.

22...♘h5
The knight has to retreat, asking the g3-bishop some questions.

23.fxg6
A must. From here on in, my position somehow starts gradually improving, as Wesley loses his decisiveness. Something radical would be more practical. 23...♘xg3!? would have been a good option here, inducing more trades. But I felt I would still have practical chances.

23...hxg6 24.♕g2
I have consolidated somewhat.

24...♔h7
...♗f4!? was an idea, now or later.

25.♖ad1
Also possible was 25.e5, but a good rule of thumb is to deploy the a1-rook before starting any action. Here it

'Winning by pinning.' Anish Giri has played 47.♖g2!, 'a high-class move' according to commentator Peter Leko, and Wesley So understands that he is going to lose the game and his one-point lead.

wasn't at all necessary, but in 99 out of 100 cases it is.

25...♖ae8 Another slow move, and since it is useful – why not?

26.a3
A decent practical decision, giving back the move (and potentially preventing ...♗b4 so as not to have the a2-pawn hanging at some point).

26...♗xg3?!
Not the best way to release the tension. Sending a piece to f4 felt more practical. 26...♗f4! was strong, and even the counter-intuitive 26...♘f4!? made sense to me. After 27.♗xf4 ♗xf4 White will somehow find it hard to advance, despite the beautiful knight on f3.

27.fxg3 ♕d6 This only gets in the way of the e5 push.

28.♔h2!
Not allowing him to provoke me – 28.e5 would be met by 28...♕d5!, when Black takes control of some key light squares.

28...♖e7 29.♖d2 We are both playing the waiting game.

29...♔g7?
But this is wrong. Now 30.e5! can no longer be met by 30...♕d5, and the knight on h5 also feels a little off. Better was 29...♔g7!?, looking for a better future for the knight.

30.e5! An excellent moment to strike, as 30...♕d5? runs into 31.exf6+!, forcing the king to f6.

30...♕d7 31.♖e4
Sending the rook over to h4. This might be a bit too much, but in a rapid game... why not? Things have turned around already, and White is clearly starting to finally have some fun.

31...♕d5? A big mistake, possibly on account of missing 33.♖e5!.
He should have gone for 31...f5 32.♖h4, when after 32...f4, 33.♖xh5! was my plan, but when I noticed Black had 32...♕d5!, I realized that things were still far from easy,

because Black keeps the game going. White would have to start playing slowly now: 33.♖e2!?, intending ♕f2 and possibly ♘g5. Black has no clear way to improve his position at this point, with the knight stuck on h5.
32.exf6+! The king should obviously be invited to the centre.
32...♔xf6

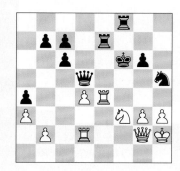

33.♖e5! If I had traded on e7, Black would have breathed a sigh of relief, having traded a set of rooks and perhaps finding shelter for the king

on the queenside with ...♔d8. Here, though, White has a huge outpost for the rook and a dominant position. The combination of the king on f6 and the knight on h5 is not pretty.
33...♕d7

This is the start of a new phase in the game, to wit my incredibly shaky conversion. I have to say it would have been hard to win more narrowly than I ended up winning it. At the end of the day, though, I managed.
34.♖g5

This is also winning, but there were more powerful options.
For instance, 34.♘h4!, intending ♕e4, wins on the spot.

34...♕d6

I felt that 34...♕e8!? would have been a more practical defence, but objectively Black is lost everywhere.

35.♖f2

The human way of playing. It was hard to imagine Black make any other move than ...♔g7 here.

35...♔g7

35...♖e6! would have been far, far more resilient, but it is a move you just don't make and besides, Black would lose even then.

36.♘h4

Going for material and basically forcing a win.

36...♖e6

Giving up an exchange is the best Black can do at this point.

37.♘f5+ ♖xf5 38.♖fxf5 ♕xd4

White is completely winning.

39.♖g4 ♕d6!

Black's position is totally hopeless, but this brilliant trap confused me completely. 40.♖xh5 would obviously run into 40...♕d3 now, and realizing

that my rook retreat from f5 will no longer be with tempo (as opposed to after 39...♕d3 40.♖f3!) I got a bit upset. Very strange, because with such an edge, there is absolutely no need for any tempi.

40.♖f2 ♖e3 41.♖e2 ♖d3 42.♕f2

I should write a book called *Winning fast and slow*. This game would definitely end up in the chapter 'Slow'.

42...c5 43.♖g5

Crushing would be 43.♕f5, but this also wins, of course.

43...c4 44.♖ge5

I thought this would be mate, but Black pulls off a semi-miracle.

44...♘xg3!

Suddenly there is no way to checkmate the king.

45.♖e7+ ♔h6 46.♕f8+ ♔g5

The king is chilling on g5. Fortunately, there is still a way to win, although I'd have to say that for me to end up in this situation, with the win hanging by a thin thread, was quite remarkable.

47.♖g2!

Winning by pinning.

47...♖e3

This loses trivially.
47...♖d2 felt like the best practical shot, as it sets up an amusing trap – 48.♖xd2?! ♘f1++!!, but 48.♖f7! leads to a completely winning endgame.

CHESS BOOM LEADS TO SHORTAGE OF CHESSBOARDS

BEREND VONK

47...♔h4 would also be more resilient: 48.♖h7+ ♘h5+ 49.♔xd6 ♖xh3+! (the point) 50.♔g1 cxd6, but Black is still utterly lost after 51.♖xg6, e.g. 51...b5 52.♔f2 d5 53.♖g1 d4 54.♖d7 ♖h2+ 55.♔g2 ♖xg2+ 56.♔xg2 d3 57.♔f3, and White will win all the pawns.

48.♖f7!

The g3-knight is pinned and will be lost.

48...♕d1 49.♖f1 ♕d3 50.♖f4

Black resigned. Mate is inevitable.

■ ■ ■

In the second semi-final set, the speedy Nepo made it to the brink of the final by winning a very nervy game in which Carlsen's attempt to squeeze something from next to nothing backfired, as the Norwegian was again in extreme time pressure. Needing to win both remaining games on command, that old Magnus magic reappeared. First, playing White, Ian overlooked a chance to force a repetition and then succumbed to sudden complications. Then Carlsen forced 'overtime' tiebreaks by following up with a remarkably easy win.

What followed was very hard to understand. The first blitz game was an immense token torture session, in which Magnus first pressed with black in a ♖+♘ v ♖ ending, then defended ♖ v ♘ after blundering his rook to a mouse-slip. Normal enough in this kind of event, I suppose? But what followed was not the way to crown a comeback we've come to know from the champ.

Magnus Carlsen
Ian Nepomniachtchi
Magnus Carlsen Invitational
2021 (sf 3.2)

position after 27.♕xb5

The bizarre course of this game forced me to pose a blunt question to Magnus. I assume that somewhere around here is where he felt he had technical control, with Black's splintered pawn structure signalling a long and painful day at the office.

27...♖c7?!

The active 27...♕f5 28.♕xb7 ♖c2 was objectively better, when Black's activity provides some compensation for the pawn.

28.♕b6? 28.♖a8+ ♔g7 29.♖d8 should result in a decisive edge.

28...♕e7

29.♕a5?!

I found this move a bit of a startler, and a visible signal that Magnus was still not quite in gear – getting the queen to d6 is a dream achievement for Black, as the back rank worries allow for a serious exchange of activity levels, and White's apparently eternal plus has more or less evaporated now.

29.♕h6 ♕d8 30.♖b1 looks like the natural way to keep up lasting pressure, even if engines aren't too perturbed. Now White no longer has a way to gang up on any of the potential target pawns in the enemy camp.

29...♕d6 30.♖b1 ♔g7 31.♕b5 b6 32.♕d3 ♕e6 33.♕a6 ♕d6 34.♕e2 ♕g6 35.♖a1 ♕e4 36.♕b5 ♕e6 37.♕b4 ♖c4 38.♕b1 ♕c6 39.♕f5 ♖c1+ 40.♖xc1 ♕xc1+ 41.♔h2 ♕c7+

42.g3

Magnus typically insists on embarking on a path to prolong the fight. On a good day, this is business as usual, on a bad day it will get written off as the first step on the road to a tilt.

42...hxg3+ 43.♔g2 ♕d8 44.♔xg3 b5 45.♕b1 ♕d6+ 46.♔f3 b4 47.♕b3 ♕f6+ 48.♔g2 ♕d6 49.♔g1 f6 50.♔g2 ♕b6 51.h4 gxh4 52.♔h3 ♕b5 53.♔xh4 ♔f7 54.♔g4 ♔e6 55.♔f4 ♕c4 56.♕a4 b3 57.♕e8+ ♔d6 58.♕b8+ ♔c6

59.♔f5??

59.♔f3 ♕b5 60.♕e8+ ♔b6 61.♕d8+ was still fine for White.

59...♕b5

60.♕c8+

The crucial difference now is that after 60.♕e8+ ♔b6 61.♕d8+ ♔b7 62.♕e7+ ♔c8 63.♕f8+ ♔c7

ANALYSIS DIAGRAM

White's king position prevents further checks (if 64.♕e7+, then 64...♕d7+), and the b-pawn becomes lethal.

60...♔b6 61.♕b8+ ♔a5 62.♕a7+ ♔b4 63.♕a1 ♕e2 64.♔e6 b2 65.♕a6 ♕xa6+ 0-1.

Speaking to Magnus after the event, I asked him how on earth that happened? That game was the least Magnus thing I can ever remember seeing.

'What I can say is that I cracked – I cracked under the pressure.'

Really? After that comeback? It's not like you felt superhuman or something?

'No, not at all. Somehow, getting into the tiebreak, I didn't feel like I was particularly coming from a position of strength. I felt that I had played so unbelievably badly on that day

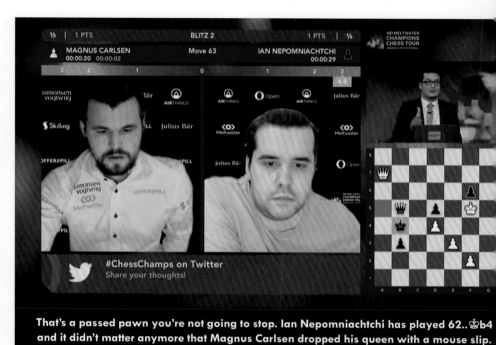

That's a passed pawn you're not going to stop. Ian Nepomniachtchi has played 62..♔b4 and it didn't matter anymore that Magnus Carlsen dropped his queen with a mouse slip.

overall, and I would almost say – *especially* in that first black game that I needed to win – I made so many questionable decisions there early on, it was bugging me as I played. I felt like everything I was doing was wrong there. In general, I'm not the best in these must-win situations or must-draw situations at all.

'I'm by far at my best when I can just play normally. Actually, I'm not so bad from a position of strength, but from a position of weakness I'm not that great. Then the second game... That was just absolute capitulation on his part. I had to make one sort of decent decision the whole game. So while I was relieved to

actually get there, I didn't feel like I had done anything special. And I felt that the way he capitulated in that second game told me that he was already getting ready for the blitz, and we would have a completely new match on our hands.

'(In the tie-break game above) everything was sort of going according to plan. Then, at some point, I couldn't find a way to make progress. At first I thought I had to be close to technically winning, then I couldn't find a way to make progress, and then it was obviously a draw, and I continued to play for a win.

'And the moment that I realized that he was better and I had to play for a draw – I just froze. I just completely froze, and I could sense that he was getting more and more confident. And I just completely and utterly folded – which spoke of the fact that I wasn't in a great state of mind at all during that couple of days.'

Is that your conclusion – just bad days?
'Obviously this doesn't happen in a vacuum. Clearly it has something to do with me not handling the pressure that well these days.'

Magnus Carlsen: 'I'm not the best in these must-win situations or must-draw situations at all. I'm by far at my best when I can just play normally'

Meanwhile, Anish needed only a draw to keep his second match level and eliminate Wesley. But the Dutch number one began to drift, and was quietly getting annoyed with his play. Then came a dramatic and pivotal moment.

Anish Giri
Wesley So
Magnus Carlsen Invitational
2021 (sf 2.4)

26.g4
26.♘e3!? was a solid alternative. Looking back, Anish commented: 'I felt that if I went g4, maybe I would threaten g5, maybe gxf5, if ...g6 maybe g5. I had missed a bunch of things by that point. I had missed ...♛a6, I had missed the fact that gxf5 is not really a threat.
'So ... it felt wrong, but I thought it was a practical decision at this point. More honestly, it was not a brave decision but more a consequence of a mini-tilt. I had just made a few bad moves at that point and this was another one that was no good.'

26...♛c7??
As Anish mentioned, 26...♛a6! would give Black a solid advantage, with long-term weaknesses on the light squares to exploit, and keep So's chances of forcing overtime by winning the second 'set' alive.

27.♖xe6
Wesley resigned immediately. A very curious error in reaction to presumably an unexpected move. Consistency of form seems to be the supreme challenge of the Tour's gruelling format.

A chance for consolation

The Carlsen-So match indeed took place in the last bracket – just not the gold bracket. This time their clash decided on third and fourth place. Magnus finished the event with a return to form, romping to victory in both sets, powered by a memorable start.

NOTES BY
Peter Heine Nielsen

Magnus Carlsen
Wesley So
Magnus Carlsen Invitational
2021 (final 3rd/4th 1.1)
Four Knights Opening

1.e4 e5 2.♘f3 ♘c6 3.♘c3 ♘f6 4.a4!?

Matches for third and fourth place are primarily played for the entertainment of the public, and Magnus very much tries to do this by playing this unusual move. It might be just that, but apart from being a possible tribute to the Van Foreest brothers, both of whom have played this irregular move, it does have a few hidden points...

4...♗b4
Basically, being granted a 'free move', Wesley continues as if that was indeed the case. Alternatively, flipping back the move to White, with ...a5, ...a6 or even ...h6, would also have been sensible. But such nuances will surely be covered in an upcoming Yearbook Survey!

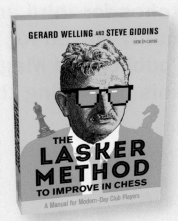

Matches for third and fourth place are primarily played for the entertainment of the public, and Magnus very much tries to do this by playing this unusual move

5.♗d3!?

Lucas has played this in the exact same position, and Magnus played it with colours reversed, and so with the pawn at a7 (a2). With Black it is seen as a way to 'get a game', avoiding simplifications, but at the cost of giving White chances of an advantage. A relevant question now is whether the pawn being on a4 here alters this fact?

5...d6 6.0-0 0-0 7.♘d5!

The a-pawn already makes itself felt! If 7...♘xd5?? 8.exd5 ♘e7 then 9.c3 wins a piece, as the bishop on b4 is trapped: 9...♗a5 10.b4 ♗b6 11.a5! being the principal and important point.

7...♗c5 8.c3 a5

Black's play is very logical. His last move prevents White's threat of b4, so now he is threatening ...♘xd5.

White's position looks somewhat over-extended, unless he would limit himself to 9.♘xf6+, seeking equality.

9.♗c2!

A very interesting move played by Lucas van Foreest against Arkadij Naiditsch in last year's Bundesliga. It ups the stakes in the sense that White threatens 10.d4, hitting the bishop on c5, while also threatening ♗g5. Naiditsch replied cautiously with 9...♗a7 10.d4 h6, but then White has a decent space advantage. Wesley plays the principled continuation:

9...♘xd5 10.exd5 ♘e7 11.♗g5!? h6

Again, So stays principled. Instead, 11...♗f5 12.♗xf5 ♘xf5 13.♕h5 h6 14.♘e4 would allow White to keep a small initiative without complications. Now, however, Magnus is really forced to show his hand.

12.d4 ♗b6

White's position indeed looks over-extended. His centre is weak and it seems that the 'primitive' threats on the kingside were too easily parried. Well...

13.♘h7! ♖e8 14.♘f6+!! gxf6 15.♕h5

White has sacrificed a full piece, but crippled Black's pawn structure around his king. The computer, however, is unimpressed, showing 0.00, as if nothing has happened....

15...e4!?

A very logical move, its point being that 16.♗xe4 allows 16...f5, and when the white bishop returns to d3 or c2 then 17...♘g6! is possible, since the g6-square is no longer attacked by the white bishop. As a result, Black is just in time to consolidate.

15...♕d7 is simply met by 16.h3, and if 15...f5 16.♗xh6 ♘xd5, both 17.♗b3 and 17.♗g5 give White a promising attack.

16.♖e1!

The big point, and still kind of within his preparation – at least it was noted that the engines like the move. One can even argue that the value of 4. a4 depends on this tactical resource ☺.

Magnus Carlsen: 'Even though it was something I knew about from preparation, I was smiling from ear to ear after that game. I was really happy.'

LENNART OOTES

that after 20...fxg5 21.♕g6+ ♔f8 22.♗xd5 cxd5 23.♖h3!, despite Black being two pieces up and White only attacking with two pieces, there is nothing Black can do to avoid an immediate mate.

20...♔f8 21.♕g6 f4

After, for example, 21...♗e6, 22.♗xd5, followed by 23.♗xf6, wins. Wesley protects the h3-square, but Magnus, in true online-style and basically without pausing, lashed out:

22.♗h6+! ♔e7 23.♕h7+!

The elegant check that So had missed. In this manner, White keeps the f5-square protected and so 23...♔e6 24.♖xe4 is mate! If Magnus's aim was to entertain the public, he certainly succeeded. And it won him the game as well.

■ ■ ■

A delightful game, and one that Carlsen agreed gave him a lot of satisfaction. 'Yes, even though, as I mentioned, the whole ♘f6 thing was something that I knew about from preparation. I just had to find a couple of over-the-board moves after that, but yeah, I was smiling from ear to ear after that game. I was really happy. I think, regardless of what you have achieved in chess, if you crush one of the best players in the world and he resigns on move... I don't know, 20 or something, with mate in two – if that doesn't make you feel anything, then you should probably take a good hard look or re-evaluate some things. I am very hard on myself in general, but that, yeah, that was fun.'

Now 16...♗f5 looks logical, but then, after 17.♖e3 ♗g6 18.♖g3! (not 18.♕xh6? ♘f5!), White's attack is good enough for at least a draw, which anyway was the best that Black could achieve in the position, despite being a piece up. So's move might look logical, but it loses.

16...f5?

17.♗xh6! The main point of removing Black's h6-pawn is that ♗g5 becomes an unstoppable threat, with mating motives appearing on the dark squares around the very lonely black king.

17...♘xd5 18.♗g5 f6

In case of 18...♕d7, the most beautiful win is 19.♖e3!?, with the idea of

19...♘xe3 20.♗f6!, mating.

19.♗b3

19...c6 If 19...fxg5 then 20.♕g6+!, followed by 21.♗xd5, wins trivially.

20.♖e3!

A stunning move, the point being

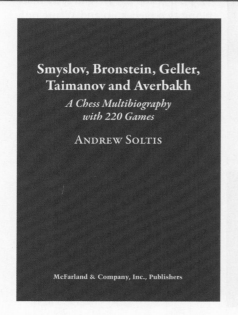
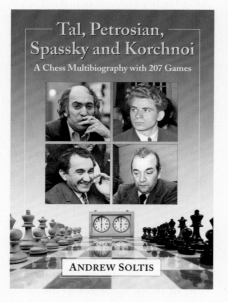
When speaking to Magnus, I also took the opportunity to ask him about the challenges ahead and a couple of other things. With the World Championship match to take place in Dubai in November and the second half of the Candidates tournament to be played in April, he must be thinking about his next Challenger.

Magnus Carlsen: 'I still feel like I'm the best, there's no doubt about that – and I just have to prove it'

You saw three of the Candidates here, and of course Anish eliminated the two current leaders, Vachier-Lagrave and Nepomniachtchi. Did you make any interesting observations from watching them play and what they played?

'There was very, very little new there in terms of Ian (Nepomniachtchi) and Maxime (Vachier-Lagrave). Ian played well against me, but he didn't show me anything new. He plays the same way he always plays. He plays quickly and he does some things very well and other things less well. No surprises there. In terms of Maxime, it is a lot of the same.

'Now Anish was very strong in this tournament, especially in terms of preparation. I think he was by far the best. He doesn't have any history, though, or much history I should say. I was told that in his interview after the tournament, he was kind of dismissive about the idea that winning this tournament was a big deal to him. I would say that this is by far the biggest tournament that he has ever won. So there is that.'

I saw an interview of his in which he said that you had a relationship of non-mutual respect, with him having great respect for you, and you not having any for him. Does that get a reaction?

'I would say that I definitely respect huge parts of his game. And that he would respect me even more goes without saying (long chuckle).'

Any final thoughts about the current drought of victories then? Clearly not age, you don't feel any slower now just because of a number?

'I think that there is no reason why my peaks should be any lower. I think I have every chance of getting back to the level that I had in 2019. I don't feel any different at all. But the margin for error is a little bit lower without that kind of youthful full energy.

'That means that I think, inevitably, motivation is going to be an issue, and there are going to be some ups and downs. It's certainly bothering me that I'm not winning any of the events that I am playing at the moment. Saying anything else would be a pretty blatant lie.

'But I'm trying to look at this last tournament as a massive encouragement, since my general level of play was pretty good and I really only had one bad match. Otherwise I think I did well. Obviously, the context of the match against Wesley was different from what it usually is, but I think it was probably still an important win, especially because of the way in which it happened, because he is certainly going to be a strong competitor on that front in the future.

'So right now I'm feeling pretty good. It's not like I wake up and I have a different opinion of my chess compared to others than I did a few months ago. I still feel like I'm the best, there's no doubt about that – and I just have to prove it. Obviously, you can't keep saying that forever! But for the moment I feel pretty confident that this is not going to be a lasting thing at all.'

Centre stage

The final featured another duel of many levels, with Anish Giri once again having to juggle winning the event with the tricky business of balancing revealing future intentions – Ian Nepomniachtchi is his next opponent when the Candidates finally resumes in the second half of April.

What little serious over-the-board chess there has been during Covid times indicates that this pairing was a clash of in-form players; Anish's Tata Steel result was impressive – on the other hand, Ian ended 2020 by winning the Russian Super Final.

The first day fascinated, as the pair went toe-to-toe in four Sicilians, all four games ending in hard-fought draws, but with one near miss by Anish in Game 1.

The next day was very similar, but with landed punches.

NOTES BY
Anish Giri

Anish Giri
Ian Nepomniachtchi
Magnus Carlsen Invitational
2021 (final 2.2)
Sicilian Defence, Taimanov Variation

1.e4 c5 2.♘f3 e6 3.d4 cxd4 4.♘xd4 ♘c6 5.♘c3 ♛c7

Ian Nepomniachtchi had been going for Taimanov Sicilians a lot in the tournament, keeping, or at least pretending to keep, his main weapon

the Najdorf for the Candidates Tournament. In the preliminary stage, I lost to him with white after 5...a6, but in the knockout stage Ian kept going for 5...♛c7, which is the more traditional move order.

6.♗e3 a6 7.g4

The day before, in our first match of two, I took on c6, which is another rare line. This time, too, we quickly left the main paths. Like the Najdorf, the Taimanov offers White a lot of different variations on moves 6 and 7. The main moves here are 7.♛d2, which is the traditional English Attack, and the ever-trendy 7.♛f3, which I faced a lot back in my Taimanov days around 2015.

7...h6!? A novelty, but the computers don't dislike this move too much and it didn't come as a shocker. The main move here is the standard 7...b5. With 7...h6 Black wants to slow down the g5 push.

8.h4 Slowly but surely preparing g5.
8...♘f6 Alternatively, he could have gone for 8...b5 here.

9.♘xc6 White needs to prepare g5 and this, followed by ♛f3, serves that

exact purpose. The more standard Sicilian idea of 9.♖g1 would run into 9...♗b4!, when Black appears to get quite some counterplay in the centre, since the e4-pawn would be hanging..

9...bxc6 10.♛f3

Protecting the h1-rook and threatening g5, but also preparing 0-0-0.

10...d5

After a ♘xc6 bxc6 trade in such positions, the normal question is whether to continue with ...d5 or to play ...♖b8 first. Very nuanced.

11.g5 hxg5 12.hxg5 ♖xh1 13.♛xh1 ♘g4

A tempo move.

14.♗d2

I had prepared this far, but hadn't studied this particular position in much depth, since both sides had plenty of deviations earlier on. The move Ian played here, set me thinking.

14...♗b7

A natural move, preparing queenside castling and reinforcing the d5-pawn. I recalled the variations with the bishop going to d7, which is far less human, obviously.

15.♛h3

I had seen this idea in similar positions. The queen is doing a fine job controlling the third rank and pointing at the e6-pawn.

15.♗e2 was my first instinct, but after the knight retreat I didn't find a good follow-up. After 15...♘e5 the engine points out the very strong 16.♗e3!, while 16.f4?! ♘g6! and 16.0-0-0 d4! do indeed give Black adequate counterplay.

Now White just stops d4 and wants to castle queenside, with a great position, seeing that Black can't advance his central pawns with ...c5/...d4, and is left without any follow-up here.

15...♘e5

Ian Nepomniachtchi inflicted Anish Giri's only loss in the first half of the Candidates tournament, but had to bow to the Dutchman in the final of the Magnus Carlsen Invitational

16.0-0-0 I couldn't get 16.f4 ♘g6 17.f5 exf5 18.exf5 to work in view of the queen check on e5.

16...d4 17.♘b1

I liked 17.♘a4 better optically, but in some lines I didn't want my knight to be attacked with ...c5/ ...♗c6. Now I want to push f4-f5 and Black has to play really well to prevent his position from crumbling.

17...c5?!

Black should have done some preven-

tive thinking and taken the threat of f4 more seriously.

17...♘g6! doesn't look exciting, but having stopped the f4 push, Black gets to keep his important e6-pawn intact: 18.♘a3 c5. I would be quite happy with the c4-square for my knight here, but Black has the important f4-square under firm control and his position is quite solid.

18.f4

18...♘c6?

Black goes for the 'better'-looking square, but this is just losing. The solution at this point was almost impossible to find, although someone as gifted as Ian could perhaps have pulled it off on a better day – or if he had taken some more time here.

Black should have played 18...♘g6!.

He is anyway losing the battle for the light squares, so he should at least fight for the dark ones. 19.f5 ♘e5!. This is counter-intuitive, since the e6-pawn seemed key, but it was necessary to dig deeper here. 20.fxe6. In view of the reply, this may not even be the best move.

ANALYSIS DIAGRAM

20...♗c8!!. A beautiful idea. For a pawn, Black has regained control of some key squares: e5 and, very importantly, c4. 21.exf7+ ♕xf7 22.♕g3 ♘d6, with dynamic equality. White had some better options on move 20, though.

18...♘d7 was the move I had expected, and I had seen the following line: 19.g6 ♗xe4 (19...c4!! would still keep the game exciting) 20.gxf7+

☗xf7 21.♗c4, and Black's position collapses: 21...♗d5 22.♗xd5 exd5 23.♕h5+!. This check from the side, and not 23.♕f5+? ♘f6!, is important. The d5-pawn will fall and White will win.

19.g6!
The e6-pawn is doomed. Black now tries to get his king to safety.
19...0-0-0 20.gxf7 ♕xf7 21.♗c4
♔b8 The king does remain quite safe on the queenside, but having lost a pawn for nothing and with no control over the e5- and c4-squares, Black's position is hopeless.
22.♗xe6 ♕c7 23.♗c4 ♔a7

This was the last important moment in the game. I thought for a while, and then realized that I should stop wasting my time, since every move is equally winning and all I had to do was avoid time-trouble and miracles.
24.♘a3
The knight will eventually get to c4.
24...♘b4 The knight is sitting pretty on b4, but it can't offer any counterplay on its own.
25.♖e1 ♗e7 26.♔b1
Black is helpless.
26...♖e8 27.e5 ♗d8 28.♗b3

Now the knight finally makes its grand entrance via c4. Black is dead lost.
28...g5 29.♘c4
The knight is heading towards d6.
29...gxf4 30.♗xf4
As some Soviet commentators used to say, White has the pawn and the compensation.
30...♘d5 31.♗d2 ♕g7 32.♘d6
♖h8 33.♕e6 ♗h4

MC Invitational 2021 (KO finals)			
Quarter Finals			
Carlsen-Aronian	2½-½	2-1	
Nakamura-Nepomniachtchi	2-2	½-2½	
So-Firouzja	2½-½	2½-½	
Giri-Vachier-Lagrave	2-2	3-1	
Semi-Finals			
Nepomniachtchi-Carlsen	2½-1½	1½-2½	1½-½
Giri-So	2½-1½	2½-1½	
Final 3rd-4th place			
Carlsen-So	3-1	2-1	
Final			
Giri-Nepomniachtchi	2-2	2-2	2-0

Trying some last-ditch tricks, but first of all, the 34.♘xb7 complications work, and White can just move the rook over.
34.♖c1 ♘c7 35.♕c4
The c5-pawn is now a target as well.
35...♕xe5 36.♘f7 ♕h2 37.♕xc5+ ♔b8 38.♕xd4
It's a matter of taste now, since everything wins.
38...♖f8 39.♗f4 ♗g3 40.♗xg3 ♕xg3 41.♕b4

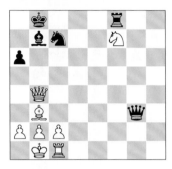

Black resigned. He is two pawns down, with a weak king, but there's also the concrete issue of not being able to deal with ♘d6.

■ ■ ■

Ian struck back on demand in the final game, cashing in as Black on a very dynamic performance in another Sicilian, this time a 3.♗b5 rather than the previous battlefield of the Taimanov. Although it would be easy for Giri to second-guess himself into distraction after this result, he instead took solace – inspired by Ian! If Nepo could stumble violently and still beat Magnus in the semis, then they would both be very aware that Ian's comeback here could be equally hollow.

In the first blitz tie-break game, another moment of high drama arose, and in the interview I had with him after the event, Anish recounted the astonishing number of things that went into a quick and fateful decision. He went into immense detail, providing a revealing catalogue of the rush of ingredients that go into an extreme high-stakes blitz decision at the Tour level, plus a dose of philosophy.

Anish Giri
Ian Nepomniachtchi
Magnus Carlsen Invitational 2021 (final 3.1)

1.e4 c5 2.♘f3 e6 3.c3 d5 4.e5 ♘c6 5.d4 ♗d7 6.♗e2 ♘ge7 7.♘a3 cxd4 8.cxd4 ♘g6 9.♘c2 f6 10.exf6 gxf6 11.0-0 ♗d6 12.g3 h5 13.♗d3 ♘ce7 14.♘e3 h4 15.♘g4 ♔f7 16.♖e1 ♕f8

Anish Giri: '(The sacrifice I played here is) actually very easy to explain. I wasn't familiar with this whole business, 9...f6, I took 10.exf6 and he took with the g-pawn. I thought this was a very interesting decision, and here he's got control over the central squares and has this potential for a slow kingside attack.

'So after ...h5-h4 I have ♘g4. I realized, OK, maybe his king is also a bit weak, maybe I have some ♘h6+ coming. He prevents it with 16...♕f8, which is very strong. He took some time, so I saw it before he played it, that it would be very strong, but at least I gained some time.

'Then I realized: because the centre is closed and there was a slightly similar game, Aryan Tari against Firouzja, from Norway Chess, you have this structure: d5, e6, f6, which controls the e5-square – and White at some point just has no plan forward.

'You can't challenge this pawn structure, and the guy is just going to slowly bring stuff toward the g-file – ...♕g7 ...♖g8. These moves are easy, and of course he's going to make

them. And I have to come up with some counterplay. Because on the queenside there is no counterplay, there is no pawn break.

'I quickly realized that I didn't even know objectively – but practically speaking I was actually in a very desperate strategical situation. If I play something like ♗d2, ♖c1 – pointless moves that you can just make – he's going to play ...♕g7, ♖g8, then he's going to sac a knight on f4, similarly to what he did against Magnus a few days ago. He beat him there (*see the first Carlsen-Nepo position above from the semi-final*).

'So I realized I needed a desperate measure. Now the thing is, I have a sac: ♘f6, ♘g5, ♘e5, ♗g5 – I have a few sacs.

'I cannot think now and choose what is better. I'm never going to realize which one is better. I don't have the time for it. I'm not a computer. I know that I have to sac something,

Champions Chess Tour – standings

Wesley So	140	$85,000
Magnus Carlsen	135	$65,000
Teimour Radjabov	108	$78,500
Anish Giri	105	$75,000
Ian Nepomniachtchi	83	$60,000
Levon Aronian	67	$60,000
Maxime Vachier-Lagrave	54	$46,500
Hikaru Nakamura	40	$30,000
Daniil Dubov	23	$25,000
Alireza Firouzja	6	$12,500
Jan-Krzysztof Duda	3	$7,500
David Anton	0	$12,500
Alexander Grischuk	0	$7,500
Sergey Karjakin	0	$7,500
Ding Liren	0	$5,000
Vidit Gujrathi	0	$5,000
Pentala Harikrishna	0	$5,000
Shakhriyar Mamedyarov	0	$5,000
Nils Grandelius	0	$5,000
Jorden van Foreest	0	$5,000
Alan Pichot	0	$5,000
Le Quang Liem	0	$2,500
Peter Svidler	0	$2,500
Sam Shankland	0	$2,500
Leinier Dominguez	0	$2,500
Matthias Bluebaum	0	$2,500

somehow. Otherwise I am going to lose without a fight. Practically. Or at least I will have to be defensive.

'So then I just pick a random one and I picked 17.♘fe5+, because I saw that I would get a pawn to e5, and I've got the f6-square. Maybe I could stick a piece there.

'I missed a bunch of things, there is ...♗b4, there is ...♗c6, ...d4, but I just felt that sacrificing was a better practical choice.

> **'The good thing is that, at that point, some blitz experience helped. I knew first of all, you cannot think forever'**

'The good thing is that, at that point, some blitz experience helped. I knew first of all, you cannot think forever. Secondly, you cannot play slowly because you're going to lose, and yeah, I had bad luck with picking the wrong sac, but good luck that it worked out.

'So it was not really a stylistic choice, it was just how I think about chess, and my understanding is that I cannot play it slowly. If I could do something without saccing a piece, which I thought was good, I would definitely have done it. I just thought that it was the best decision at that point.'

17.♘fe5+?

17.♗g5! was the eventual analytical

And it's game over after 32.♖g4. Anish Giri and Ian Nepomniachtchi clearly have different thoughts as they look at the final position of the first tiebreak game that essentially decided the final.

verdict, if we still have eventualities in the engine age. Their well-known 0.00 assessment is reached after 17...fxg5 18.♘xg5+ ♚g8 19.♘xe6 ♕f7 20.♘g5 ♕f8, with a repetition of position.

17...fxe5 18.dxe5 ♗c5

Anish mentioned 18...♗b4 as a strong alternative.

19.♗g5 hxg3 20.hxg3 ♗c6 21.♖c1

21.♕f3+!? ♚g8 and inserting a minor piece into f6 gives White ongoing murky compensation.

21...d4 22.♗e4 ♗xe4 23.♖xe4 ♘f5

24.♕a4

I can't help wondering whether Ian was considering 24.♗f6 here, when 24...♖h7 looks like the harmonious response. If 24...♖g8 then 25.♕f3,

with the idea of following up with ♚g2, and ♖h1 looks like it could be annoying. If so, could it have set the stage for what happened in some way?

24...♖c8 25.♗f6

25...♖h7??

25...♖g8 26.♚g2 ♕e8 27.♕b3 ♕c6 28.♕f3 ♕d5 29.♖h1 is hopeless for

Anish racked up a hefty payday, an elite tournament victory and a guaranteed berth in the Tour final. Can it get better?

White if you are a machine, but might still stir up trouble in a blitz game.
26.♕d7+!

Suddenly the looseness of the c8-rook is fatal, and quick, pragmatic mess creation gets maximum reward. Black goes from clearly better to unable to resist in an instant.

26...♘ge7 27.♗xe7 ♕xe7

If 27...♘xe7 28.♖f4+.

28.♕xc8 ♗b6 29.♘f6 ♖g7 30.♕h8 d3 31.♕h5+

31...♖g6

31...♚f8 32.♖c8+ ♗d8 33.♕h8+.

32.♖g4 1-0

The second blitz game was no strain on Giri's nerves. Ian's 'surprise' opening choice was something Anish had considered before, and he emerged with something even deadlier than a large advantage – an advantage that was extremely easy for him to play at speed. Ian went down again. Anish racked up a hefty payday, an elite tournament victory, another Candidate scalp, and a guaranteed berth in the Tour final. Can it get better? We'll soon see. ∎

Anish Giri:

'I like healthy chess'

His win in the Magnus Invitational seems to have improved his chances in the Candidates Tournament. Anish Giri is on a roll, and may take his good form to Yekaterinburg. **JONATHAN TISDALL** wants to know more about the Dutchman. How does he work on his game? With which World Champion does he feel affinity? And while we're at it, could you name five things that make you happy?

This tournament looked like quite a commanding performance – how does the entire event strike you, looking back?

'I think you can only talk about a commanding performance in hindsight, because more often than not you have somebody playing very well, and then being knocked out at some point because of one slip.

'I really love these World Cup tournaments, these giant knock-outs. I love watching them and participating in them as well. And in every World Cup you usually have one guy who shines from the start and makes a score of 8 out of 8 or 7½ out of 8 in the first four matches – and then suddenly he has one slip-up, and he goes out. And the player who wins in the end is usually the one who was fighting from the start and got used to the rhythm of fighting. I don't think you can really talk about commanding in knockout events. In this tournament, it happened in such a way that you could say: next to Magnus, I showed good form from the preliminary.'

The big thing that struck me about the entire event is preparation. Do you have a rapid repertoire? An online repertoire? How do you handle this?

'That's very different for everyone, of course. You've got, especially in earlier times, people who, out of principle, wouldn't play anything that they normally play or have prepared. Then, at some point, rapid suddenly became a thing that also pays very well because of the Grand Chess Tour, so it would be a bit strange, when you are fighting for the kind of prizes you fight for in a normal event, to suddenly give opponents advantages.

'Once you start seeing that certain opponents are playing preparation, you wonder – wait a minute – why don't I start doing this as well? So you start copying each other a bit. That really changed the trend. These days, everybody prepares one way or another.

'What helps me is that I have already played so many of these events that the preparation accumulates. I hadn't prepared for this 1.b3 in the second tiebreak game against Nepo, but I looked at it at some point for one of the matches. At some point, I had a base called Nepo prep, then a file called Nepo prep 2, 3. I keep playing the guy, you know. Eventually, these things accumulate and you form a kind of repertoire.'

Just for rapid? Not trying to get you to give anything away...

'No, it's a good question. I would say that I treat these things differently. And there is an overlap as well, of course. When it comes to rapid, I try to be much more aware that there is little time to think. And that, of course, influences the choices.

'As a general rule, you are aiming for positions that you are more comfortable with by nature. What your natural habitat is, let's say. That is something that you discover with experience. Then you start noticing, also in blitz games, that in certain positions you play better or

'What helps me is that I have already played so many of these events that the preparation accumulates'

Anish Giri with the Predecessors volume in which Garry Kasparov looks at the career of Max Euwe. "The story nowadays that players are universal is slightly exaggerated.'

Well, maybe he's not going to do that at the Candidates, because obviously that would slightly defeat the purpose. It's unlikely that he would announce it beforehand. At the same time, he was very well prepared.

'And honestly, let's say he wanted to play the Najdorf, why wouldn't he play it? These days, things have really changed quite a bit. Everybody knows that the Najdorf is fine. The only question is whether you will anticipate what your opponent does, and it is all about the small details.

'For example, let's say you play the Najdorf. If you get hit by some new idea, you would rather get hit in a rapid tournament than in the Candidates. So it's all a question of whether you want to play your main openings or not. It's a big question, with pros and cons.

'For Ian to say: "Yeah, I was not playing my prep, while, I'm sorry, going for the most forcing lines in the ♗g5 Najdorf every game..." I think he had never rehearsed so many files in a rapid tournament before as he did here.

'I understand that. I think players sometimes get into this mood of preparation, this routine of looking at stuff with engines, repeating the files, and I think me and Ian were in this mood. He was playing his prep. Whether he played his main opening or not, we will see.'

What do you take away from having eliminated both of the leaders from the Candidates here?
'I'll try to make it a little bit bigger than it is, and pretend that now I have a tremendous psychological edge, but it's clear, of course, that if I were on the receiving end, I would downplay it. When it's positive, you take it as a sign of confidence and so on, but when it's negative, I'm sure they'll just shrug it off and say it was just rapid and nobody cares.'

worse, and you try to adjust to that somehow. Of course, you're also constantly trying to get out of your comfort zone. Otherwise you can't grow.

'But I feel that in rapid and blitz, you should stay in your comfort zone more than you have to in classical chess. Because in classical chess, you have more time to find solutions that are counter-intuitive. So, for me there is some difference. I tend to go for things that I find easier to handle.'

With that kind of consideration in mind, and with the Candidates coming up, I imagine you're keeping a very close eye on and constantly interpreting what MVL and Ian are doing in terms of the opening.
'It's a sort of poker game, yeah.'

So when you hear that Nepo says: 'It will be nice to play a tournament where I'm not purposely not playing any of my openings,' you have a definite reaction to that.
'Yeah, that was a very good one. Obviously, he was very well prepared for the rapid event. All these things he did in the Taimanov, for example; they're clearly not out of the blue.

Anish Giri's relief after he won his game against Kirill Alekseenko in Round 6 of the Candidates tournament. When the players return to Yekaterinburg we will find out who benefited from the 12-month interruption and who didn't.

What do you think of the effects of this delay – has the rest of the Candidates become a second mini-event?

'Yeah, for sure. It is so hard, very often, for players to change the flow of an event. There is so much advice; you should have a walk, especially old Soviet stories. A very proud Russian trainer, he said that this woman was playing a world championship match and doing badly, then I came and I told her to go skiing with me, and after that she started playing well.

'I am strongly against drinking in any form for any reason. I myself never drink, but some people say alcohol or going out, having a party... There even was a story that Magnus, after he lost to Karjakin – in the match – he went out to some party? I don't know if it really happened, but it could have.

'So many ways. But here you postpone an event for a whole year, where people have a chance to fully recover. I mean, Ding Liren no longer remembers the pain he endured there. Fabiano, he comes fully back with a streak of good results, while he really struggled there. I think Fabiano would never have won the tournament if it had continued. He was just off. And now he is one of the favourites.'

So you think it favours everyone but the leaders?

'No, I think it favours Ian as well. I think Ian is a very tilty individual and he lost the last game. And if you see his interviews... he was unhappy, coughing. He was complaining every interview. Of course he always does, but there it was a bit more genuine. Surely favours him quite a bit.

'It is definitely horrible for MVL, because now he seems to be off form, whereas there, he was completely on a roll. Let me put it this way, the French players that I know, many of them, but particularly the French players that I know, they are so superstitious. They believe in a lucky card, and in jinxes. And it seemed so perfect for him, he got invited [replacing Radjabov – JT] and he was winning

at the start, and now he's leading, and he beat the leader. Everything is great, so it seemed like *destiny*.

'The odds have clearly gone down. I'm sure that if you are a betting website, the odds on him winning are much lower now than then.

'For me, I am in much better shape now, but at the same time, of course, I would much rather have played Nepo the day after he lost to Maxime, when he was still complaining, than now. Not to mention chess-specific things. I don't know if Ian had another opening for 1.e4, but now he can play the Taimanov or the Najdorf or whatever he wants.

'Yeah, things have really changed a lot, and it had a tremendous effect, and you cannot deny that. But nobody is to blame or anything, at least not by me. But you cannot say that nothing has changed; that would be outrageous. Of course things changed.'

Can you describe Anish Giri's playing style and what famous player he reminds you of?

'That's funny. Garry Kasparov is really into World Champions and chess history, and the first question he asked me when we had a brief session, was "Which World Champion do you

think you resemble?". Which is really putting you on the spot when you're a kid, and Garry Kasparov is asking. You want to appear modest. But it's a good question.

'The story nowadays that players are universal is slightly exaggerated. Everybody still has certain stylistic elements. One of the things I would mention on the positive side is that I have a lot of interest in opening preparation, so I am usually well-prepared. Another positive thing I would say is that I have pretty good endgame technique – even on the bad side, but usually on the good side – although I think that having good endgame technique in good positions is a trait of a modern chess player.

'I think this is something you really need to have as a top player now, because of the theory being so advanced, and players all being so strong. If you don't make a difference in these slightly better positions, you will miss out on so many points.

'I think I am reasonable there, too, but so are most top players. I think I like healthy chess, and I don't consciously gamble. I always try to take the correct decision and do the right thing.'

What did you tell Kasparov?

'I think I said Euwe. And he said (gruffly) "Why?" And I was like – oh no, was this the wrong answer? But he just said: Why? I said I thought he was also into openings and quite well-prepared. Kasparov says gruffly: "OK, OK..." He didn't dislike it.

'Now I would do better at that question, because I know more about myself and other World Champions. At the time, I probably thought it natural, because Euwe was Dutch.

'Ah, Petrosian. Maybe he brought it up, or I did. Petrosian was known for prophylactic thinking, and minimizing his opponent's counterplay. And I have a pretty good sense of danger, which can of course backfire, in the sense that I see danger when there isn't really any. This is the flip side. If you work with the clichés, I would mostly pick Petrosian.'

This reminds me a lot of something I feel compelled to ask – I saw you telling a very interesting and shocking story about Petrosian nearly giving up chess (because of constant criticism about being 'drawish'). Especially in our social media times: Whose opinion is worth caring about?

'I think what people say is very important, because what it boils down to for everyone is their own sense of approval. And I would guess that your own sense of approval owes a lot to your upbringing and your parents and those who approved of you as a kid. Parents, teachers...

'At some point you establish your own sense of approval, which is kind of shaky, and very sensitive. That's why there are so many clips about body-shaming and such, this whole phenomenon of people judging you on Instagram and all that. The reason it matters is that sometimes you read something that slightly resonates with you, and then some doubt might rise in the back of your mind.

'Bringing it back to chess, if... let's say that there is a thought in the back of my mind that bothers me, that maybe I don't win enough tournaments or

something like that, and I read that as well, written just once by some anonymous person somewhere. That could suddenly really get deep into your head, because it actually mirrored your own thoughts, which were deep, but have now been brought to the surface.

'That is why these things can really matter. But at this moment in time, I would say that I am not too insecure. But there have been different moments.'

What's the source of your chess motivation?

'Great question. I think that is one of my strengths. It is there by default. There is no source needed. It is so deep and internal at this point, I can't remember

when it wasn't there. I was always chasing chess, as far as I can remember. There have been periods, usually when I played reasonably well, when I might get a bit complacent sometimes, a little less driven to do things I don't like doing, but I love working on chess so much that I don't need motivation.

'You need motivation to do things that you don't like. The easiest example is to wake up, say before nine o'clock. Because I just don't want to do that. But if I tell myself that if I wake up at six in the morning for a week, it will help me win a tournament because it will make my character stronger, I am going to do it.

'Once I was very pissed off after Shamkir, because I played so badly there. I told myself I am going to take a cold shower every day from now on, and I played in China immediately and I went to some ice sauna. Once I told myself that I was going to win the tournament by doing that, it was

easy to be motivated – and I in fact won the tournament. It was quite remarkable.

'But working on chess is something I love, and to do something you love, you don't need motivation. So in that sense I am very, very fortunate. And many colleagues who have worked with me would be really astonished, and ask me how I managed to work so hard, and I didn't want to tell them. Because I feel I am on average a lazy kind of guy, but the secret is that I really like it and they don't. It's kind of unfair. I am not really more motivated or organized. Just that for me it's what I love, it's in my comfort zone, so it's no effort.'

'Having good endgame technique in good positions is a trait of a modern chess player. If you don't make a difference in these slightly better positions, you will miss out on so many points'

I noticed this sign that's always behind you ('Do more of what makes you happy'). So I thought I had to ask you for five things that make you happy – your family can only count as one.

'The sign is a gift from my sister-in-law, just a small present; something to hang on a nail. It has really no deep meaning for me. But OK, I endorse this message.

'Family for sure of course. I'm thinking about whether I should split chess – let me say, chess as one thing. And let me say, winning as a separate thing because you can still do chess but not win, and it's still happiness, but not as much (laughs).

'Let me think (long pause). Good food! You'd be surprised the impact food has on me. And... let's just say a good walk. Because a good walk can also make one happy. I just described my perfect tournament routine for you basically!' ■

Long before Beth Harmon and *The Queen's Gambit* made chess cool – and women crushing pretentious men at chess even cooler – there was a group of 'radical' women in California who were balking at the male chauvinistic conventions of the day and collecting scalps along the way. The undisputed 'queen' of this band of rebels was LaVieve Mae Hines. **BRUCE MONSON** presents the story of easily the strongest American female chess player you've never heard of. And presents a shocking solution to the mystery of her sudden disappearance at age 37.

America's forgotten women's champion

Just as the Olympic Games of Paris 1924 and Amsterdam 1928 had inspired the formation of chess tournaments (and the creation of FIDE!) in their backdrops, the 1932 Summer Olympics, held in Los Angeles, inspired the Pasadena 'Olympic' Chess Congress of 1932. It featured then World Champion Alexander Alekhine and a contingent of rising American stars such as Kashdan, Reshevsky, Fine, Dake and Steiner, who convened at the Maryland Hotel in Pasadena to fight for honours in what would be California's first 'international' tournament. The contest, won by Alekhine (albeit narrowly), was memorable for many reasons, but perhaps most for an event that occurred *off* the chessboard before the tournament began.

LaVieve Hines (left) faces Mary Bain at the Pasadena tournament. In second row Alma Wolff is playing Marion Fox.
Standing: Tournament Director Alex Taylor, Elizabeth Hillman and Marie Hinchman.

Along with Alekhine, Capablanca had also been invited to play at Pasadena, but Alekhine famously – some would say infamously – demanded an additional $2000 if Capablanca was allowed to play, a fee the tournament committee could not afford, thus resulting in Capablanca being unceremoniously *disinvited*!

While researching this tournament back in 2008 for my biographical work on the Hungarian-American player, Herman Steiner, my focus was naturally on the main tournament. But there were many other events at the congress such as team matches, a women's competition and even a sky match played in a blimp above

Los Angeles! Evidently only the blimp could compete with Alekhine

The amazing story and mystery of LaVieve Mae Hines

for media attention, since the other events received sparse coverage in the newspaper accounts.

The women's tournament was won in an 8-0 rout by a woman I had never heard of named LaVieve Hines. The California organ, *The Chess Reporter*,

also included a group photo of the ladies but did not name the players, except for the 'Champion', shown sitting. I did not recognize any of the faces in the photo except the man, tournament director Alex Tayor. It later turned out that two ladies in the photo were not in the tournament

---

Bruce Monson first drew attention to LaVieve Mae Hines in the book on the 1932 Pasadena Chess Congress that was published by Caissa Editions in 2011. He remained fascinated by Hines and new discoveries he made in the past years are included in this article.

She was fluent in three languages and five dialects and was said to have 'a voice range of two and one-half octaves and capable of upper F with a clear tone'

at all. And one lady who *was* in the tournament was not in the photo!

Surely, this was a tale of mere beginners, right? Mass confusion about *en passant*, castling and all that. I was about to skip to the next 'critical' detail concerning the main event when I saw a blurb in one of the newspaper articles showing the final standings in the women's tournament. One name stood out. In fourth place out of six competitors was Mary Bain!

Surely not *the* Mary Bain? The first American woman to represent the US in an international chess competition? The same Mary Bain who caused a sensation at the Hungarian Chess Club in New York 1924 when she drew her game against the great Geza Maroczy during his simul there? The same Mary Bain who defeated José Capablanca in just 11 moves (!) only a few months later in the simul he gave at the Hollywood Chess Club in April 1933? The same Mary Bain who would finish in fifth place at the Women's World Championships at Stockholm in 1937?

Of course, it *was* her!

The question at hand is how in the world could a player of Mary's skills only manage fourth place among a small group of unknown California 'woodpushers'?

And more intriguingly, who was this LaVieve Hines lady?

The Pasadena Chess Club

It turns out the women who competed in the Pasadena tournament were far from rank beginners. Each of the women had at least five years of experience playing against not only women, but the best male players in the club. The Pasadena Chess Club promoted women's chess heavily and took pride in its policy of not segregating women from men, whether in competitive events or in electing their club officers. In fact, the club president was Mrs. Elizabeth 'Betty' Hillman. 'Women are seldom made welcome at chess clubs,' wrote CCLA

President Clara Cameron in a 1929 letter to the Los Angeles Times, 'and are too proud to go where they are not wanted, and the Pasadena club, which caters so to women, should be congratulated for abandoning the caveman theory of inferiority of women.'

It was conventional knowledge that male members of the club and visitors alike needed to check their egos at the door!

Their bravado did not go unnoticed by the media. In an article from the Pasadena Star-News in 1929, a feature photo-op story on the women headlined: Women Invade Scientific World Of Chess – Pasadena Team is Formed to Compete With Best Men Players City Can Produce.

Long before Beth Harmon made chess cool for millions of Netflix junkies around the world binge-watching *The Queen's Gambit*, these 'radical' women were balking at the

A publicity photo from a 1904 playbill advertising LaVieve Hines as 'The Greatest Child Actress in the World'.

male chauvinistic conventions of the day and collecting scalps along the way. LaVieve Mae Hines was their undisputed 'queen' and easily the strongest American female chess player you've never heard of. And if her results are any indication (almost exclusively against the strongest male players on the West Coast), she is likely the strongest female player the US had ever seen up to that time. So how is it that her name could be utterly unknown?

Finding LaVieve's family proved to be a tough nut to crack. The woman valued her privacy, a trait shared by her family. The rewards were worth the effort. Her archives were a veritable treasure trove of amazing artefacts: photos, documents, trophies and hand-written treaties from a surprising source. As always proves the case, however, it was the memories from family that were the greatest treasures!

Born in Buffalo, New York, in 1896 to a stock speculating father and an overbearing mother, LaVieve ('Net Net' as she was called by family) was driven headlong toward stardom from an early age. She was lauded as a child prodigy on violin and nearly as skilled at piano, having studied under famed composers Moritz Moskowski (piano) and Joseph Joachim (violin), the latter of whom was the close friend of Johannes Brahms who dedicated his Violin Concerto to the Hungarian violinist.

But her talents extended well beyond classical music. She was an astute student of Russian ballet, tap dancing and other forms of dance. She was fluent in three languages and five dialects and, as one Buffalo writer put it, she was said to have 'a voice range of two and one-half octaves and capable of upper F with a clear tone.' By age seven she was already under management of B.M. Garfield and his famous 'Buster Brown' company. An early playbill from 1904 headlined her as 'The Greatest Child Actress In The World'. Her destiny was clear. Or so it would seem. She was to be Shirley Temple before there was a Shirley Temple. But that didn't happen.

In 1913 William Hines, LaVieve's father, lost most of the family fortune after investing heavily in a failing Canadian mining company. The loss put a strain on not only William's financial stability but also his marriage to Amelia, LaVieve's mother.

There was also the Great War that got underway in 1914. Wars change everything and as US entry became imminent in 1917 the insecurities of life started to hit home for Amelia who saw the lifestyle she had envisaged for herself and her children slipping away. She began to press William relentlessly to move the family to Hollywood so LaVieve could finally realize her potential (and by proxy, Amelia's) on the silver screen. William refused, but Amelia was steadfast in her determination and in 1918 she, LaVieve (now 20) and son James packed up abruptly and left for California.

William was devastated and died of melancholy four years later. His anger is evident in his last will and testament: 'I give and bequeath to my wife Amelia M. Hines, my daughter LaVieve M. Hines and my son James Wesley Hines each the sum of Five Dollars; I also give and bequeath to my daughter LaVieve M. Hines one Stainer violin which is now in her possession with the hope that its music will cheer and brighten her life. No other provision is made for my said wife or children for the reason that they have all deserted me without provocation.'

They would contest the will on the grounds that William was under psychiatric care and incapable of making sound decisions, though in the end the matter was moot since there was so little remaining of the estate.

As for LaVieve's movie career... well, Hollywood is fickle. Aside from a life that could be characterized as somewhere between *Mommy Dearest* and *What Ever Happened to Baby Jane?*, the closest LaVieve came to film in Hollywood was a few gigs modelling women's fashion in the early 1920s for the *Los Angeles Herald*. Reality soon set in and she fell back on her musical talents, eventually getting full-time work with the Pasadena Symphony as a violinist. Amelia gave piano lessons.

Flamboyant and quite funny

By any standard LaVieve was an eccentric woman. She was fanatical about her appearance, rarely appearing in public without one of her exotic dresses. She often went to great lengths to conceal her real age, even on official census reports. According to family she was 'cute, flamboyant and quite funny, with a playful sense of humour.' She was also sharp-witted, outspoken and contemptuous of authority, particularly of arrogant men who looked down their noses at others.

One *Los Angeles Times* chess column from 1931 printed one of her quips about the sterner sex: 'Men aren't so bad if they are chessmen – You can generally get them to do as you wish.' And after crushing the Pasadena Chess Club champion, Alex Taylor, in a game she was quoted as saying, 'Just another one of those games where a man plays and pays.'

It's not clear when LaVieve learned chess, but it's thought by family that she was taught the game by her father while still a young girl in Buffalo. What *is* clear is that in 1928 when the vacationing National Chess Federation president, Maurice Kuhns, 'discovered' the group of chess players meeting daily in Pasadena's Central Park and formed them into an official club (Pasadena Chess Club), LaVieve Hines was among them and she was already a strong player.

Alekhine in Pictureland

In the Spring of 1929 Alexander Alekhine, still basking in his new role as World Champion, made his first of three visits to California where he was warmly received. LaVieve was among his biggest fans, as well as one of his most determined opponents. It's clear that she had already earned the respect of many men in the Los Angeles area. *The Pasadena Star-News* did a story on her, noting her plans to match wits with the World Champion. *The Los Angeles Times* chess column even notes that Alekhine 'had been told of this young lady's prowess and the champion's frequent hesitation at her board indicated that he respected [the] same.'

The game itself isn't LaVieve's best performance. But it wasn't a disaster either, and in the three games she would eventually play against Alekhine she improved in each.

Her second encounter came in August, 1932. This time LaVieve was ready to scrap.

Alexander Alekhine
LaVieve Hines
Simultaneous Exhibition – Los Angeles Athletic Club – August 9, 1932
1.d4 ♘f6 2.c4 e6 3.♘c3 ♗b4 4.♕c2 d5 5.cxd5 exd5 6.♗g5 c6 7.e3 ♗g4 8.♗d3 ♘bd7 9.♘e2 ♗e7 10.♘g3 h6 11.♗xf6 ♘xf6 12.♗f5 ♗d6 13.♗xg4 ♘xg4 14.♘f5 ♗f8 15.0-0-0 g6 16.♘g3 ♗g7 17.♔b1 a5?
A bit too ambitious, allowing White time to break in the centre. LaVieve had played the opening well and after 17...0-0 Black is at least equal, if not better.
18.e4

18...h5!

Impressive. LaVieve recognizes her mistake and regroups in truly modern fashion, threatening to push to h4 with counterplay against White's knight while also clearing h6 for her own knight to reroute to f5.

19.h3 ♘h6 20.exd5 cxd5 21.♖he1+ ♔f8 22.♕b3 h4 23.♘ge2 ♘f5

Seeing that the d5-pawn is falling, LaVieve gets her knight active.

24.♘xd5 b5!

Having lost a pawn, LaVieve offers another. What most impresses is her sense of urgency, realizing she must generate threats at all cost. Soon Alekhine will be compelled to sacrifice the exchange to quell the chaos.

25.♕xb5 ♖b8 26.♕c5+ ♔g8 27.♘ec3 ♔h7 28.♖e4 ♖c8 29.♕b5?

Alekhine blinks. 29.♕b6 is good for White, but perhaps he feared his queen getting stranded in left field.

29...♘d6 30.♕d3 ♘xe4 31.♕xe4 ♖e8 32.♕f4

32...a4!

Objectively, the quiet defence of the f7-pawn with 32...♔g8 was best (the engines *love* Black here!), but the move chosen by LaVieve was by far the more psychologically annoying move. Alekhine had hoped to reduce the tension, but LaVieve immediately found a way to inject more venom. She is outplaying the World Champion!

33.a3

Alekhine likely didn't give much thought to 33.♕xf7 since 33...a3! wreaks havoc!

33...♖b8 34.♘b4 ♕b6 35.♕xh4+ ♔g8 36.♘cd5 ♕e6 37.♕f4 ♕e4+?

A surprising mistake that must have eased Alekhine's nerves considerably. After 37...♕e2! 38.♘c3 ♕c4 Black keeps the pressure on. Even so, all is not lost.

38.♕xe4 ♖xe4 39.♘c6 ♖be8 40.♘e3 ♗h6! 41.d5

41...♗g5?

The losing move. White's d-pawn looks scary, but after 41...♗xe3! 42.fxe3 ♖xe3 the position is completely equal since the seemingly winning 43.d6? actually wins for Black in study-like fashion after 43...♖e1 44.♖xe1 ♖xe1+ 45.♔c2 ♖e6! when the pawn cannot advance since the knight can be captured with check!

42.d6 ♗d8 43.d7 ♖f8 44.♘d5 ♖e6 45.♘db4 f6 46.♔a2

And with no counterplay prospects, Miss Hines resigned.

After the game Alekhine paused to congratulate LaVieve on her play, even in a losing effort, to which LaVieve playfully responded, 'What do you mean by annoying me for 46 moves!'

Expanding her horizons

In 1930 LaVieve was awarded the title of Pacific Coast Women's Champion. Though only an honorary title, it was warranted since there were no official women's tournaments at that time and what female players she did contend with were well below her skill level.

By 1931 LaVieve had joined the Beverly Hills Chess Club where some of the strongest players in the Southland congregated, including state champion Harry Borochow, Irving Spero and George 'Pat' Patterson. By her own account she joined the club because of 'the opportunity it gave her to meet the many state, city and interstate champions and foreign experts who reside in Hollywood and are active in chess.'

If LaVieve's affront to the Beverly Hills club was her way of testing herself, then it was a resounding success. In the main club championship LaVieve was the only woman in the field. It was her first real tournament and included some of the top players in the club, including Henry MacMahon whom she defeated. She finished 4th 'just outside of prize winners', but earned the respect of her peers.

Then came the Lindley Memorial Tournament in honour of the recently deceased Dr. Charles L. Lindley, one of the founders of the Beverly Hills Chess Club. Again, she was the only woman in the field. Her remarkable score of 9½-½ stunned even her staunchest supporters while also removing all doubt from her detractors. The performance even sparked yet another feature article on her, this time in the *Los Angeles Evening Express* with a photo and headline: 'Female Intuition Bests Masculine Logic at Chess'.

It is unfortunate that none of LaVieve's games survive from these events. Like most of her games they were missing from her personal archives and the chess publications

Alexander Alekhine and LaVieve Hines in a photo taken in August 1933 when the World Champion stayed at her home in Pasadena for some days.

the black pieces against his favourite opening, the Vienna!

Harry Borochow
LaVieve Hines
'Impromptu Game' – Beverly Hills Chess Club, 1931(?) – Vienna Game

1.e4 e5 2.♘c3 ♘f6 3.f4 d5 4.fxe5 ♘xe4 5.♘f3 ♗b4 6.♕e2 ♗xc3 7.bxc3 0-0 8.♕e3 ♗g4!

This move evidently caught Borochow off guard as he goes wrong immediately. In her notebook LaVieve also mentions 8...♘c6 as another line she had been investigating, evidently as preparation specifically for Borochow.

9.c4 ♗xf3! 10.♕xf3

In hindsight 10.gxf3 ♕h4+ 11.♔e2 ♘g3+ 12.hxg3 ♕xh1 13.cxd5, giving up the exchange for a strong pawn centre, was the better option.

10...♘c6 11.cxd5? Amazingly, White is lost after this. Necessary was 11.♗b2 with only a small edge for Black.

11...♕xd5 12.♗d3

12...f5 Natural and strong. However, both of them missed the tactical resource 12...♘xe5! 13.♕xe4 ♘xd3+ 14.♕xd3 (otherwise a rook lands on the newly opened e-file) 14...♕e5+, winning the rook.

13.exf6 ♖ae8 14.0-0 ♕d4+?

LaVieve's one real mistake in an otherwise brilliant game. The immediate 14...♖xf6 15.♗xe4 ♕d4+ 16.♕e3 ♖xf1+ 17.♔xf1 ♖f8+ 18.♔e2 ♕xa1 gives Black a winning material advantage.

15.♔h1?

---

maintained the status quo for not publishing men's losses to women. There are, however, numerous reports of her scoring wins and draws against the top ranking players in the region, such as Irving Spero (the former Ohio state champion whom she 'beat in 26 moves'), George 'Pat' Patterson (Los Angeles champion), and even state champion Harry Borochow. Later she would also score draws in simultaneous exhibitions against Alekhine, Kashdan and Dake.

From 1930-1932 LaVieve herself gave four simultaneous exhibitions, mostly as fundraisers to support the Pasadena Congress. She played against both male and female opponents and was noted for her rapid play and confidence. Her final tally of +32 -4 =1 stands as a credit to her ability at this form of play. It is also notable that with the exception of Mary Bain all of her opponents from the 1932 Pasadena Chess Congress

had played boards against her in one or more of her simultaneous exhibitions and lost.

Dismantling the state champion

Among LaVieve's personal archives she did have a few game scores and position fragments, including one she was obviously proud of, a spectacular win against Harry Borochow. Borochow was a strong master, around 2350-2400 strength and at the height of his skills in the 1930s. He won the California state championship three times and most likely would have won many more were it not for the arrival of Herman Steiner in 1932. The event is not given, or even a date, though it was most likely a casual game played at the Beverly Hills Chess Club sometime in 1931. The game is significant not only because of the manner in which she dismantles the sitting state champion, but she does so with

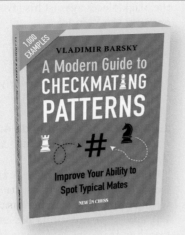
Undoubtedly hoping LaVieve would fall for 15...♕xa1?? when 16.f7+ wins on the spot. After 15.♕e3! ♕xa1 16.♗c4+ ♔h8 17.f7! ♖e7 18.♗a3 ♕e5 19.d4! ♘xd4 20.♗xe7 ♕xe7 21.♕xd4 ♘d6 22.♗b3 White would have survived the worst.

15...♖xf6 16.c3

16...♘f2+! Sufficient also was 16...♖xf3 17.cxd4 ♖xd3, but LaVieve seeks a more elegant solution.
17.♖xf2 ♕xd3! And White resigned.

First US Women's Champion?

In lieu of the string of accomplishments LaVieve had amassed, it seems almost a let-down to speak of her winning the 'women's tournament' at the Pasadena Congress as the apex of her chess career. She simply outclassed the field, probably by 400-600 points by modern rating standards. The only woman who was thought to be even a remote threat was Mary Bain. But that proved not to be the case. Clearly, she was head and shoulders above everyone else, Mary included.

In fact, LaVieve had intended to forego the women's event altogether and play in the Minor Tournament which included several expert calibre players from around the country. To locals, this was hardly a surprise since it was conventional knowledge that she was 'the equal of many of the strongest chess-playing men in California.' But it turns out there was great interest in a showdown between LaVieve and Mary Bain and she agreed to play in the women's event.

There is a strong argument that LaVieve should be recognized as the first US women's champion based on merit or 'acclamation'. It must be remembered that there was no official process for crowning a 'US Champion' for women in 1932 and there would *not* be for another five years. But that doesn't mean people weren't talking about it. Just two days before the tournament began Douglas Houghton, in his *Pasadena Star-News* column, specifically refers to LaVieve as 'U.S.A. women's championship challenger', inferring that the winner would have earned such a claim.

The United States Chess Federation lists the first US Women's champion as Adele Rivero, based on a tournament played among the segregated 'women's group' at the Marshall Chess Club in 1937. Notably, Mary Bain played in that tournament, finishing a close 2nd despite fighting the flu. However, the first 'official' championship was held the following year in 1938, ultimately won by Mona Karff. Critically, not one of the ladies from Pasadena appears to have been invited, least of all LaVieve Hines!

In contrast, the Pasadena women's tournament not only included Mary Bain, but it easily met or exceeded what minimal standards would later be applied to the New York events. Representation was coast-to-coast, it was a double round-robin event played with clocks under tournament rules, overseen by a tournament director, and the average strength of the players is indicated by the fact that Mary Bain finished in the middle of the pack.

To my knowledge LaVieve never explicitly claimed the title of US women's champion, but the notion was certainly inferred by her contemporaries. In fact, it was conventional knowledge that she was a 'competitor' who was 'the equal of many of the strongest chess-playing men in California'. This fact alone tells us a lot. But the most compelling argument is a remarkable endorsement by the sitting World Champion, Alexander Alekhine!

Alekhine, guest and coach

Prior to the Pasadena Congress Alekhine spent several days with LaVieve, residing at her home in Pasadena. This was not a romantic encounter, although given Alekhine's known propensity for older women it is interesting to contemplate his thoughts about LaVieve's mother, Amelia, who also resided at the same residence.

During this time Alekhine shared with LaVieve all of his games and analysis from the recently concluded London tournament of 1932. He also included games from previous events against the likes of Capablanca, Nimzowitsch, Rubinstein and others. In all, there are twenty-two annotated games enshrined within her blue 'Scholastic Composition' notebook, along with dozens of newspaper clippings and photos. Clearly, LaVieve was reverent, pointing out herself that the words written within were scribed in 'Dr. Alekhine's own handwriting' as if they were sacred scrolls rescued from the Dead Sea.

I can't begin to express the thrill it was to physically hold these items. All the more so as LaVieve's nephew, then in his eighties, entrusted me (and the US Mail service!) with these relics. Sadly, James passed away in 2013, but his memories of LaVieve were invaluable.

In the accompanying photo you see a sample from LaVieve's notebook, showing Alekhine's brilliancy prize game against Koltanowski at the London International Tournament of 1932.

As if that were not enough, LaVieve also notes that Alekhine was 'coaching her' for the upcoming women's tournament at the Congress and gives some of the opening variations that he had suggested for her.

Among LaVieve's artefacts was also a photo of Alekhine with an

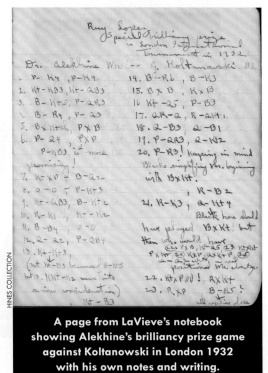

A page from LaVieve's notebook showing Alekhine's brilliancy prize game against Koltanowski in London 1932 with his own notes and writing.

HINES COLLECTION

inscribed note to her that read: *To the future American chess womens (sic) champion. Sincerely, A. Alekhin 14, Aug. 1932*

Of course, such a title for women did not yet exist, but in Alekhine's mind LaVieve was a shoe-in for the honour. He would reiterate this point in his remarks at the closing ceremonies for the Pasadena Chess Congress where he said LaVieve was 'the foremost woman chessist of the United States'.

What is an endorsement by the World Champion worth? Four days following the Pasadena tournament LaVieve would meet Alekhine in their third and final encounter.

Alexander Alekhine
LaVieve Hines
26 Board Simul – Los Angeles Athletic Club – September 2, 1932
1.e4 e5 2.♘f3 ♘c6 3.♗b5 d6 4.d4 ♗d7 5.♗xc6 ♗xc6 6.♘c3 ♘f6 7.dxe5 ♘xe4 8.♘xe4 ♗xe4 9.exd6 ♗xd6 LaVieve has emerged from the opening with the two bishops and a slight lead in develop-

ment against the foremost openings expert on the planet.
10.0-0 0-0 11.♖e1 ♖e8 12.♗g5 ♕c8 13.♘d4 ♗c5 14.c3 ♗g6 15.♖xe8+ ♕xe8 16.♕e1 Now clearly heading for the draw.
16...♕e4 17.♕xe4 ♗xe4 18.♖e1 ♖e8 19.f3 ♗c6 20.♖xe8+ ♗xe8 21.♗e3 ♗xd4 Draw.

That LaVieve was happy with the result is exhibited in the fact that she posed with the final position on the board along with her Pasadena Congress victory cup. The game is further evidence that she had the skills to match the claims.

The IT-Factor

What set LaVieve apart from almost all other women had as much to do with her attitude as with her skills on the board. Her confidence was unshakable and she didn't buy into the chauvinistic convention that women are intellectually inferior to men. 'Women', she said, 'could play chess equally as well as men if they were not psychologically beaten before they started.' In another article she extrapolates further, noting that women could not only be 'as great or better players than men if only they would apply themselves', but women are not using their best asset, 'women's intuition', which she attributes to much of her success. 'A good intuitional player', she says, 'can beat a good logical player with surprising frequency.'

Whether or not LaVieve's views on women's intuition holds up is really of no consequence. The fact that she scoffed at the idea of male superiority in chess put her in a class by herself, and not only for 1930s America. During the US Women's Championship in 1946 all the players, which included Gisela Gresser and Mary Bain, were polled on the question of male dominance and each of them admitted outright that men were better players than women. The reason? Emotionalism. 'Even those cool, capable women chess champs', said Edith Weart, 'can't eliminate their natural emotionalism which does not blend with chess playing'.

Gisela Gresser, the regal 9-time US Women's Champion, had a different take. She said the reason men are better is that 'Women are too intelligent. They have more important things to do than play chess. To be a really great chess player you have to give up your whole life to it.'

According to family, LaVieve did *everything* as if her 'whole life depended on it.' Nothing half-way. She clearly possessed both the disposition and the capacity for hard work. That's just who she was.

There can be little doubt that had LaVieve continued playing the future dominance of American women's chess by Gisela Gresser and Mona Karff would have looked much different. But LaVieve did not go on to greater things in chess. In fact, shortly after the Pasadena Congress she literally seems to disappear off the face of the planet! After around mid-1933 there is not another mention of her in chess, nor for that matter in anything.

The Girl that Got Away...
So what happened? And more, why should we care? It turns out both questions have the same answer.

I thought she must have settled down, gotten married, had children. Life. Sometimes promising chess talents just move on with realities that extend beyond a 64-square board. Had she moved back to New York or London or Paris, perhaps playing in orchestras with the Piatigorskys and Rubinsteins of the world? Had she died?

None were the case. LaVieve Hines lived to be 101 years old! After moving to Pasadena in 1918 she and her mother lived together in the same house at 1814 Maple Street until Amelia's death in 1943, and then she remained there until aged 90 when she had to be moved to a nursing home after a bad fall off a ladder.

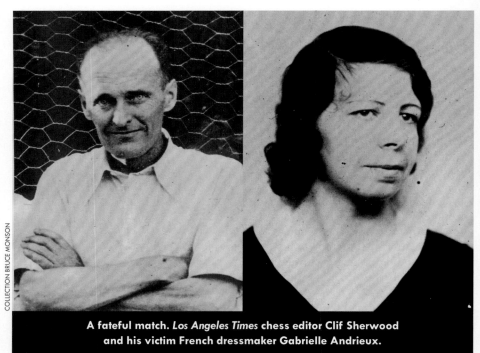

A fateful match. *Los Angeles Times* chess editor Clif Sherwood and his victim French dressmaker Gabrielle Andrieux.

She was never married and never had children. She did have a male 'companion' after Amelia died, but with separate rooms and no romantic inclinations, at least not on her part. In fact when she was 98 years old she confessed to her nephew that she was 'still a virgin, and proud of that'.

So what gives? What could have happened that would cause this firecracker of a woman to withdraw so suddenly – and completely – from chess and society? Interestingly, for family this has always been a mystery, though it was thought that it had something to do with Amelia and the power she held over LaVieve. Perhaps. But maybe there was something else.

The White Blackbird
It turns out there was one man who aggressively injected himself into LaVieve's life over a three-year period. A man who was widely lauded for his weekly chess column in the *Los Angeles Times*, but on June 19, 1933 wrote his name in the annals of chess infamy when he murdered Gabrielle Andrieux, a young French girl who had shunned his marriage proposals. His name was Clif Sherwood.

The same *Los Angeles Times* Sherwood worked for ramped up the

hyperbole in their headline the next morning: Checkmate!

And underneath: 'Death, with immutable fingers, slipped across the chess board of life yesterday afternoon and ended the game in which police were waiting to move against Clif Sherwood, 40-year-old chess expert, for the murder of Gabrielle Andrieux, French modiste, in her home at 1748 ½ Wilcox Avenue, Monday afternoon...'

On the run, Sherwood was found twelve hours later by Burbank police, seven miles away from the crime scene. He was slumped over the steering wheel in his crashed car with a single gunshot wound to the head, self-inflicted. He was taken to General Hospital where he would die early the following morning, never regaining consciousness.

It would be easy to use a tragic event such as this to sensationalize the relationship between LaVieve and Clif Sherwood, but it's not necessary. In this case reality really *is* stranger than fiction.

A singles forum
Born in 1884 in Newark, New Jersey, Clif Sherwood grew up in Westport, Connecticut. It's unknown why, but he moved to Los Angeles in

1920 and was active in chess circles almost immediately. He took a board against the 11-year-old 'Boy Wonder' Sammy Reshevsky in Los Angeles 1921 during his famous simul tour of the US. He ran the chess column in the *Los Angeles Evening Express* for one year between September 1921 and October 1922, and then started the *Los Angeles Times* chess column in October 1927. Outside chess he worked as a door-to-door salesman and other odd jobs. But he always had trouble supporting himself and changed residences frequently.

Mental illness also ran in his family. His father had been declared insane and spent the last years of his life in a sanitorium in Connecticut. Police later discovered Sherwood had *also* been committed to a sanitorium for two years, explaining his four-year absence when he abruptly left California in 1922 only to return suddenly in 1927.

That Clif suffered from manic-depressive disorder and likely other forms of mental illness is evident in his chess columns, which he frequently utilized to reveal odd points about himself or others. In one example from 1931 he cites the suicide note left by chess player Kenneth Haegg who had recently attempted suicide (and failed): 'Instinct orders "Live". But reason says "Life is senseless, therefore abandon it". Not being a fool, living in a world of fools is too great a strain.'

Sherwood's cryptic response: 'His diagnosis may have been quite correct but his method of cure not so impressive.'

Even more frequently his column was used as a singles forum in blatant attempts to drum up a romantic connection. Each week he presented a chess problem that readers would write to him with their solutions and those who got it had their names printed. Tragically, Gabrielle Andrieux's name can be found among those who 'wrote in'. Most likely she attended one of the 'social

chess for women' or other 'ladies especially invited' ruses he used to draw in women.

One woman wrote in asking whether chess players make good husbands. If there was a positive side to the tragic figure of Clif Sherwood it's the humorous self-degradation he was at times capable of, as evidenced by his response: 'The chess editor, knowing nothing about marriage and almost as much about women, ventures to guess that while the wife of a chess player might complain the first year of their married life about his staying out nights (at the club) it's a safe bet by the second year she'd complain if he didn't stay out.'

Romantic innuendo

LaVieve Hines also wrote in to his column, almost weekly. And starting in 1929 he became more and more obsessed with her. His columns mentioned her on dozens of occasions, often with some sort of romantic innuendo. And no other woman besides LaVieve received such attention. 'Miss LaVieve Hines of the Pasadena Chess Club', he notes in a column from 1929, 'is trying to organize a team of women. If they're all like Miss Hines the writer would gladly furnish a team of men to play them and enjoying (sic) losing every game.' In another, also from 1929 he says: 'Miss LaVieve Hines plays their [Pasadena Chess Club's, ed.] best

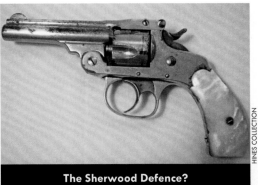

The Sherwood Defence?
LaVieve Hines' pearl-handled 1906
Smith & Wesson 'Ladysmith' handgun.

men to a standstill... but one look at this pretty young lady, and what man wouldn't let her win?'

And this from 1930: 'Miss LaVieve Hines... has been winning so regularly of late from some of the strongest men players that we have a suspicion the charming young lady's smile has something to do with it... Anyway, she needs watching: maybe that's the trouble.'

But it did not stand at mere words of infatuation. Sherwood went to some length to get involved in real life events surrounding LaVieve's chess and possibly other activities. He was a piano player and likely played up to her musical talents as well. In 1930 when LaVieve was awarded the honorary title of 'Pacific Coast woman's chess champion', who was it that appeared with her in the AP photo? Clif Sherwood. In the article it even notes that Sherwood 'has volunteered to act as a manager for her'.

In an earlier photo published in the *Pasadena Star-News* in 1929 headlined 'Pasadena Woman Will Play in Simultaneous Chess Match' [against Alekhine], Sherwood also appears with LaVieve, sitting next to her at a chessboard.

And there were many other examples, in each case with Sherwood demonstrating some gesture of infatuation toward LaVieve. And it's worth noting that among LaVieve's scrap books she had copies of all the newspaper clippings he had written about her.

Perhaps even more interesting is what is *not* in her scrapbook. While there were numerous articles in the media about Clif Sherwood's murder of Gabriella Andrieux and his subsequent suicide, there is no reference whatsoever to those events among LaVieve's papers. Naturally, she would have been shocked by the events and shunned any reference to it.

Others did the same. Under the heading 'Chess and Crime' in the July-August 1933 *The Chess Reporter*,

She disappeared from the chess arena forever. According to family she seemed happy enough, content with the solitude of music and nature, birdwatching, turtles and a curious interest in California's goldmining history

Henry MacMahon spoke collectively for the entire Southland chess community by distancing themselves from Sherwood in no uncertain terms. Several times MacMahon refers to Sherwood as a 'white blackbird', which was a turn-of-the-century term for an anomaly of nature, 'an aberrant curiosity that fascinates spectators', like Alexander Dumas' *The Black Tulip* or Horace's black swan. Which was all just another way of saying Sherwood was not one of *us*. 'Chess players', MacMahon continued, 'are proverbially honest, they're not out to do you except on the black-and-white battlefield'. He goes on to lambast the media for calling Sherwood an 'expert' at chess and reminds us that he was not, stating that chess was merely 'an escape' for Sherwood, but 'never a major interest or any kind of obsession'.

MacMahon was being disingenuous. Although Sherwood was indeed well below 'expert' strength as a player, he was quite knowledgeable about the chess world he wrote about. He had a large following of 'friends' through his chess column, including MacMahon himself who had previously praised Sherwood in *The Chess Reporter*. Sherwood was even the master of ceremonies for Alekhine's much touted simultaneous exhibition held at the Los Angeles Athletic Club in 1929.

Smith & Wesson handgun

After MacMahon poetically cleansed chess (and chess players) from any stains Sherwood might have left on our dear game, those dark memories gradually faded into the background noise. Chess went on. Even the *Los Angeles Times* chess column went on, taken over by the recent New York transplant, Herman Steiner. Club tournaments, city and state championships, simultaneous exhibitions all continued. People didn't just stop playing chess.

Except for LaVieve Hines.

After June 1933 there is no further reference to LaVieve having anything to do with chess or chess players! Not once in the next twenty years did she write in to Steiner's column with a solution to the weekly chess problem. Had she simply decided to hang up her pawns after the Pasadena Congress? Not likely. In fact, she had expressed interest in playing in the next cycle of the Southern California Championship! Family had no answer, though they thought Amelia had something to do with it. However, one artefact they shared with me is highly suggestive. It is LaVieve's pearl-handled 1906 Smith & Wesson 'Ladysmith' handgun! And she had a license to carry it. Prepared, evidently, for all threats real or imagined.

Here's what I think happened.

The murder of Gabrielle Andrieux scared the hell out of LaVieve. Seeing how close Clif Sherwood had managed to get to her she must have imagined the very real possibility that it could have been *her* lying dead, head bludgeoned and shot twice in the chest. But even that might not have been the final straw were it not for her mother, Amelia, who most likely settled the issue in no uncertain terms – *finis!*

Epilogue

In 1937 Douglas Houghton, the tireless chess promotor and editor of the chess column in the *Pasadena Star-News*, expended some effort to bring LaVieve back into chess. The timing is significant since it was about the same time that the first 'Women's National Championship' was being contested in New York. He of all people knew that any such event without LaVieve would be about as credible as someone claiming to be the United States champion in the time of Morphy. He may even have employed that same analogy. Houghton somehow convinced LaVieve (initially, at least) to perform a simultaneous exhibition at the 1937 Morphy Day festival in nearby Sierra Madre. The festival was a favourite of hers, one she had helped organize from its inception in 1930.

'Champion Returns' was the headline Houghton gave in his column. 'A feature new to the Morphy Day program will be the women's rapid-transit tourney and simultaneous exhibition by Miss LaVieve Mae Hines, Pasadena and women's champion of California. Miss Hines has been absent from the carnival for the past three years. Her return to the lists of the chess arena will be welcomed by her host of friends.'

Unfortunately, no such exhibition took place and it is doubtful whether LaVieve even attended since there is no further mention from Houghton. She disappeared from the chess arena forever. According to family she seemed happy enough, content with the solitude of music and nature, birdwatching, turtles and a curious interest in California's goldmining history. And in her final years not even her precious violin or piano held interest. Only 'Mr. Big', her childhood teddy bear, followed her to the nursing home where she died peacefully in 1997.

Inexplicably, even with all the media attention she had received in the press and the long list of great masters who knew her, talked with her and even played games against her, her name somehow drifted into oblivion and she was forgotten.

If nothing else, I hope this article will at least change that. ∎

My 100 Best Games
Jan Timman

Covers a career of more than 50 years and includes wins against Karpov, Kasparov, Kortchnoi, Smyslov, Tal, Bronstein, Larsen, Topalov, Spassky and many others.

"This is magnificent. The book is dotted with fascinating anecdotes. Timman plays in a swashbuckling style, but always underpinned with a great strategic and positional sense."
GM Daniel King, Power Play Chess

Typical Structural and Strategic Manoeuvres
Boris Zlotnik

In 2004, 12-year-old Fabiano Caruana and his entire family moved to Madrid. The Caruanas wanted to be sure that Fabiano would be tutored by the best chess trainer in the world.

And Madrid is where Boris Zlotnik lives.

Exploring the Most Difficult Challenge in Chess
Cyrus Lakdawala

"If we can see the secrets of success on how to defeat Magnus, then surely it will help our own game." – *IM Gary Lane, Chess Moves Magazine*

"One might arguably claim that this book merely reinforces just how strong Magnus is."
CHESS Magazine

"Instructive annotations, interspersed with exercises to engage the reader in the learning process."
IM John Donaldson

A Practical Guide to a Vital Skill in Chess
Merijn van Delft

"Excellent examples. Will have a major impact on your positional progress."
IM Gary Lane, Chess Moves Magazine

"A grandmaster-level skill explained in a comprehensible and readable fashion."
GM Matthew Sadler

"Masterfully discusses a vital topic, to bring your chess to the next level." – *GM Karsten Müller*

The Tactics Workbook that Also Explains All the Key Concepts
Frank Erwich

"One of the better exercise books to come out in recent years." – *IM John Donaldson*

"An extremely useful training manual. Many club players will benefit."
IM Herman Grooten, Schaaksite

"I was very impressed by the range of positions that Erwich selected." – *GM Matthew Sadler*

Vital Lessons for Every Chess Player
Jesus de la Villa

"If you've never read an endgame book before, this is the one you should start with."
GM Matthew Sadler, former British Champion

"If you really have no patience for endgames, at least read *100 Endgames You Must Know*."
Gary Walters Chess

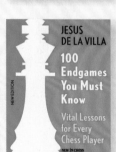

The Modern Way to Get the Upper Hand in Chess
Dmitry Kryavkin

"Kryakvin shows in a fascinating way that g2-g4 can be played in virtually every chess opening. For the aggressive club player who likes to surprise his opponent." – *Florian Jacobs, Max Euwe Center*

"A veritable potpourri of aggressive ideas to spice your White openings."
John Upham, British Chess News

How a Grandmaster Finds his Moves
Joel Benjamin

CJA 2019 Best Instructional Book

"Insightful, well-structured and it fulfills the promise of its title." – *Chess Life Magazine*

"This could go on to become one of 2019's greatest hits." – *Sean Marsh, CHESS Magazine*

"A must for every chess player and coach."
Florida Chess

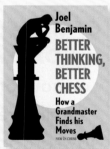

AlphaZero's Groundbreaking Chess Strategies and the Promise of AI
Matthew Sadler & Natasha Regan

2019 Averbakh-Boleslavsky Award
ECF 2019 Book of the Year

"Quite inspirational." – *Magnus Carlsen*

"Once you experience the power of these ideas in your own game, you realise how much we can learn from the playing style of AlphaZero." – *IM Stefan Kuipers*

"This is a phenomenal book." – *IM John Bartholomew*

Improve Your Skills to Overpower Your Opponents
Herman Grooten

"A highly readable account of a bamboozling art. Vital if you want to raise your rating."
IM Gary Lane, ECF Newsletter

"An excellent book for ambitious club players!"
FM Richard Vedder, Schakers.info

"Succeeds and amuses, and is truly suitable for players of all levels."
IM Frank Zeller, SCHACH Magazine

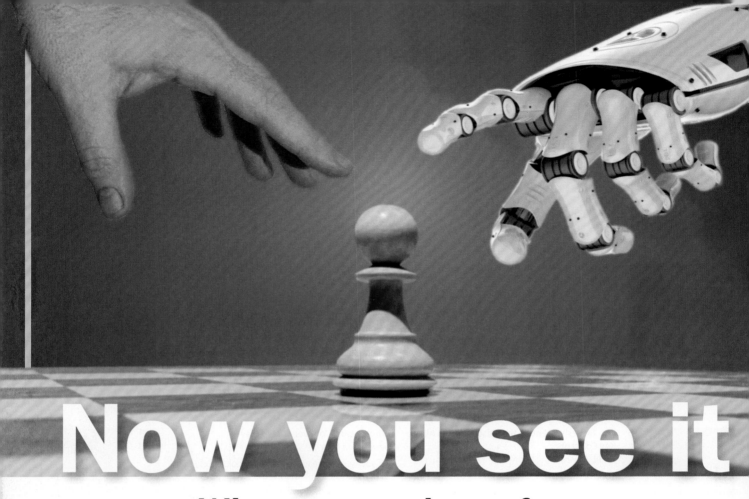

Now you see it

What we can learn from jaw-dropping engine moves

Often the plans of chess engines are so deep that they teach us nothing. **NOAM MANELLA** is fascinated by incredible computer moves that are out of this world, but in fact easy to understand. The Israeli digital mind researcher and chess author is convinced that studying such jaw-droppers will make you a stronger and more flexible chess player.

One of the most exciting areas in the world of chess right now is the connection between computers and human creativity. Human chess has always been based on common premises about right and wrong and on thinking patterns. Nowadays, many of those principles, evaluations and assumptions are tested and challenged by merciless engines. These engines, by default, also always check moves that most chess players, including the top players, may reject immediately on intuitive grounds, if they consider them at all.

In the book that I wrote together with Zeev Zohar, *Think Like A Machine* (Quality Chess, 2020), we investigated the types of jaw-dropping moves that were recommended by chess engines, but were missed by top players during their games or, in case of games from the pre-computer era, even in their analysis. During our adventurous journey we encountered crazy moves, fantastic ideas and concepts that seemed to come from another planet.

Here it is important to emphasize that we were not interested in moves connected with the apparently infinite calculating depth of engines. Such immensely deep analyses were obviously beyond human reach. What we were looking for were ideas that ran contrary to common human assumptions, habits and intuition, but that at the same time were totally within human capabilities, sometimes only one or two moves away. Once such hidden moves are revealed to us, their logic immediately becomes comprehensible.

The main contribution of chess engines is to make humans understand that there are hidden possibilities for special moves in almost any type of position. We commonly accept in chess (and life) that every rule has an exception, but now we can meet these exceptions everywhere. And so they have become a legitimate part of the 'rules'. We can call this situation 'chaorder', a hybrid of chaos and order. The chaos in our mind about right and wrong, going by the old rules, leads to a new way of looking at and diagnosing chess positions.

In our time, computers play the role that once was played by chess geniuses like Steinitz, Alekhine, Botvinnik, Polugaevsky, Tal, Petrosian and many others. Those geniuses pushed human chess thinking forward by challenging generally accepted assumptions. The amazing thing is that nowadays every child, anywhere in the world, can analyse their own games with the 'help' of an 'Alekhine' or 'Fischer'.

The study and appreciation of machine 'thinking' will enrich a player's analytical power and improve their understanding. Therefore, I invite you to dive with me into the fantastic reef of the engine's world, to spot some beautiful chess corals. The first example is taken from our book,

all the other examples are new. Take a deep breath – we are going deep. Are you ready?

The following position appeared in Alexei Shirov's celebrated book *Fire on Board* (Everyman Chess, 1997). It's an analysis diagram from the notes to his game against Oleg Nikolenko (with Black) that was played in the 1991 Soviet Championship in Moscow.

White has just played 25.♗h6!. He is a rook down and all his pieces are hanging, but Shirov nevertheless believed that his chances were better. However, before publishing his book, Shirov computer-checked the analysis and 'Fritz4 found the really astonishing **25...♕f4!!**, after which the position is about equal'.

As we can see, Fritz4, a 'primitive' engine in comparison with, say, Stockfish 13, was able to find great moves which eluded even the most talented grandmasters, as early as the 1990s (both after 25...♗xe4 26.♕xg7+ ♔e6 27.♖xf1 or 25...♕xa1 26.♕xg7+ ♔e6 27.♕e5+ ♔d7 28.♘f6+ ♔c8 29.♗f4, White wins). Now after **26.♗xf4 ♗xe4 27.♗e5 ♖g8** material is about equal and Black's king is safe.

When this position was given as an exercise to some of Israel's most talented junior players, almost no one found 25...♕f4!, even after a reasonable amount of time. There is good reason to believe that this will change in the near future. This kind of move will become more and more natural.

Noam Manella: 'Nowadays every child, anywhere in the world, can analyse their own games with the "help" of an "Alekhine" or "Fischer".'

I invite you to dive with me into the fantastic reef of the engine's world, to spot some beautiful chess corals

One move deep, but invisible

There is general agreement that the emergence of engines has improved the defensive abilities of humans. About 15 years ago, Jacob Aagaard took upon himself the task of computer-checking about 3,000 analysed combinations (taken from actual games). The outcome was astounding: about half of them had been mis-analysed. Aagaard's (2005) engine discovered hidden defences that had been overlooked by both the players and the commentators.

Humans have learned by now that even when the situation looks desperate, there is a high probability that there is an unexpected salvation waiting to be revealed.

Protected! Really?

Recently, the chess world was amazed by another stunning discovery. The following position, taken from an analysis of the game between Mark Paragua and Das Debashis at the 2012 Parsvnath Open in New Delhi, went viral on Facebook. The question was: Can Black save himself?

ANALYSIS DIAGRAM

While humans struggled to find the right answer – curiously enough, some GMs suggested 24...♖e1+, with the idea 25.♖xe1?? ♛d8!, and Black wins. But the machine just giggles with 25.♗d1!!, and sudden mate! – the machine offers, within a second, the unbelievable:

24...♛g4!!!

Straight to the most protected place on earth.

ANALYSIS DIAGRAM

Now if:
A. 25.♗xg4+ ♔g7 26.♗f5+ ♔g6 27.♗xg6 fxg6 28.♛g4 it seems that Black is lost again, but yet another miracle happens:

ANALYSIS DIAGRAM

28...♔h8! 29.♛xg6 ♗f4+ with 30...♖f8!!, and everything is protected.
B. 25.♖xg4?? ♖e1+!, followed by ...♗b4, mate.
C. 25.♛xg4 ♖g8!, and Black is OK for the third time.
D. 25.♛f6+, and Black has the amazingly winning 25...♛g6!!, which blocks the mating attack, after which Black will have too much material for the queen.

Truly amazing! 24...♛g4!!! is only a move away, with a forced and not too complicated continuation. Nevertheless, this move is beyond the horizon for most humans.

Total Chess

In the 1970s, we were introduced to a new soccer philosophy called 'Total Football', which was best represented by the Dutch national team managed by Rinus Michels in the 1974 World Cup. Total football means that the players' roles rotate during the game and that the same player can appear in various positions on the field of play. Every player had to understand the whole geometry of the whole pitch. The Dutch legend Johan Cruyff, who was nominally a centre forward, often played much deeper or on the wings, confusing the opponents.

Analogously, when we are active in one area in chess, we should be

aware of what is happening all over the board. For a human, it is hard to include in his view the complexity of the entire board, so most players tend to divide the board into 'geographical' zones: the kingside, the queenside, the centre, second and seventh rank, etc.

The common hitch is to think about each zone separately – even unconsciously. The computer, however, plays 'total football', and every square may be the most significant one, including 'neglected' areas which humans find unworthy to explore.

Wesley So – Magnus Carlsen
Opera Euro Rapid 2021 (final 2.3)
position after 16.♗b3

Here Carlsen played the noncommittal 16...exd4. Very tempting was **16...♗xh3!** but it was almost inhuman to find the only way to proceed with the attack after **17.gxh3** Now if 17...♛xh3, then White goes 18.♗xf4 ♘xf4 19.♘e3, with ideas like ♘g5 or ♗c4, and it is hard to find ways for Black to keep his attack going. However, there is **17...a4!!**

Actually, Black doesn't need his a-pawn at this stage of the game, so he can use it to win an important tempo, enabling his rooks to join the hunt of the white king at the other end of the board.

18.♗xa4

After 18.♗c4 b5! 19.♗e2 f5!! all Black's pieces are participating in the chase, for example: 20.♔h1 fxe4 21.♘g1 d5!, with a huge attack.

18...♕xh3 19.♗xf4 ♘xf4 20.♘e3 ♖ae8!

20...f5!? gives White more chances, for example: 21.♗b3+! d5 22.♘xe5! ♖f6 23.♕f3! ♖g6+ 24.♘xg6 ♕xf3 25.♘xf4 ♕xf4 26.♘g2!, with an unclear position (for a human).

21.♗b3 ♖e6!!

This is the main point behind 17...a4. Black wants to open the f-file on his own terms. By this point, a human would probably have already stopped calculating and assessed their chances intuitively.

Now let's imagine that we are the clever detective Hercule Poirot of Agatha Christie's novels and films. We have to find out is who is the 'killer'– the one who is going to checkmate the white king. Don't try to calculate – just use your attacking intuition.

The rest of the analysis is absolutely inhuman – and in fact slightly digresses from our theme – but it is truly fantastic, so stay tuned.

22.♗xe6 fxe6 23.♘g5?!

23.♘h2! is objectively better, but much less human.

23...♕h6

If Black goes 23...♕h4, then White also plays 24.♕g4!.

24.♕g4 ♖f6!

How to confront the deadly threat of ...♖g6 ?

25.♘f5!! exf5 26.exf5 ♕xg5 27.♕xg5 ♘h3+ 28.♔g2 ♘xg5 29.dxe5 ♖xf5 30.exd6 ♖xf2+ 31.♔g3

31...♔f7!!

Another machine ingenuity, a double-purpose move. The black king moves closer to the d-pawn, but, more surprising, it will play a key role in the mating net that will be wrapped unexpectedly around the white king.

32.♖ad1 ♖xb2! 33.d7 ♗b8+ 34.♔h4

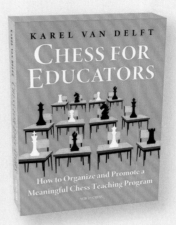
Let's imagine that we are the clever detective Hercule Poirot and that we have to find out who is the 'killer'

34...♔g6!! 35.d8♕ ♖h2+ 36.♔g4

Time to go back to Hercule Poirot and reveal the mystery. The main killer is:
35...h5 Mate.
Who would have believed after 17...a5-a4 that the attack would be finished with the h-pawn?

The idea of 'total chess' is easily associated with an offensive approach, but it also applies to a defensive way of thinking.

The next position didn't occur in the actual game. Boris Gelfand could have gone for it, but he considered it too risky.

**Analysis position from
Judit Polgar – Boris Gelfand
Khanty-Mansiysk 2009 (3.2)**

When you imagine such a position in your head, you imagine your vulnerable and shaky king one step away from the guillotine. So Gelfand avoided it and played 'safely' and eventually lost. Actually, this is natural human 'paranoia' during a tense battle. However, the machine, free of psychological worries, tells us to stay calm and not be tempted by 26...♘xf5? 27.exf5 ♕f7, because after 28.♕h4! White's attack is decisive. Instead, the machine goes for:
26...♘xb2!!
'An amazing queenside resource at a moment when the main theatre of action is on the opposite wing. Black is aiming to distract the white queen from the kingside'. (Judit Polgar, *A Game of Queens* – Quality Chess 2014).
27.♕g5!
27.♕xb2 ♘xf5 28.exf5 ♔f7!. With the white queen far away, Black has time to regroup his forces.
27...♘xd3 28.♖xg7+ ♕xg7+ 29.♗xg7 ♔xg7

The black king is exposed, but the White queen cannot do much on its own, and as a result of 26...♘xb2 Black has a dangerous passed pawn, so White has to seek a draw with 30.♕xd6.

Hidden possibilities

Every chess player has to believe that there is a hidden creative idea, just waiting to be revealed, in every position, even in apparently dull, technical positions with no adventures on the horizon. This is one of the main contributions of the

Just imagine that Boris Ivkov had spotted the amazing 35...♗f3!!

computer to human chess thinking.
Here is such a 'dull' position in which most chess players would let their creativity go to sleep. The 12th World Champion Anatoly Karpov usually felt at home in such technical positions, in which he would try to realize the advantage of the bishop pair.

**Anatoly Karpov – Boris Ivkov
Bugojno 1980
position after 35.♔h2**

White seems to have a stable advantage with no risk, while Black seemingly lacks a useful plan. In this state of mind, Karpov had just played the 'slow-motion' move 35.♔h2?. His opponent Borislav Ivkov reacted with the banal 35...♖c8, and after 20 more moves of Karpovian torture he resigned.

Had Ivkov been a modern player, he would have sought a hidden option, and might have found:

35...♗f3!!

Eyeing e2 and activating his rooks. Suddenly White's long-term edge of the bishop pair has disappeared.

36.♖xd7 36.♖f2 ♖d2! 37.♖ef1 ♗e4!, and suddenly White is the one under pressure.

36...♖xd7 37.♗b4 ♖c7!

To be followed by ...♗d5 and pressure against b3, when White is the one looking for equality.

Aronian – Vachier-Lagrave
Tbilisi World Cup 2017 (6.9)
position after 54.e6

Aronian's e- and d-pawns seem to be unstoppable. Vachier-Lagrave considered his only chance to be the 'normal' 54...♖a8?, but after 55.♖f1+ ♖f4 56.♖xf4+ ♔xf4 57.♖xa2 ♖xa2 58.e7 his position was hopeless. The engine offers a surprising twist to the plot:

54...♖aa4!! Doubling rooks is not a counter-intuitive idea, but humans are used to do it on open files rather than open ranks in the middle of the board. This strong move sets up mating threats against the white king. White is forced to use his rooks to avert those threats. As a result, he is no longer able to keep his advanced passed pawns.

55.♖f1+ And not 55.e7?? ♖g6+ 56.♔h5 ♖g5+ 57.♔h6 ♖h4, mate.

55...♖af4! 56.♖xf4+ ♖xf4 57.♖xa2 ♔xe6

With a level position.

In chess, the 'horizon' is considered as a depth beyond which one is unable to calculate. This is a proper definition for engines. For humans, the horizon may not be necessarily very deep. Sometimes we have a 'mind fog' and are unable to see what's 'under our noses' due to some unforeseen circumstances, unexpected zugzwang, for example.

In the following position, White, with only two rooks for queen and bishop, has an incredible dominating position, thanks to his protected pawn on e7. How can he break through?

Angel Quiroga – Shelev Oberoi
North American Junior 2020
position after 39...axb6

40.a3!!

40.♖2g3 ♕e5!, with no way for White to make progress without getting perpetually checked.

40...c5 41.a4!! Zugzwang! Black must free the g5-square.

41...h5

41...♕d7 42.♖f7!, winning.
41...♕e5 42.♖f7!, winning.
41...♗f5 42.♖g8+!, winning.

42.♖2g5!

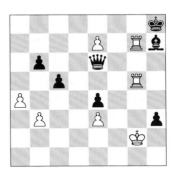

Continuing to execute the zugzwang idea. Now White controls e5 and Black is dominated from all sides, but it ain't over till it's over. Black has his own devilish zugzwang trap.

42...h4 42...♕d7 43.♖f7! ♕d1+ 44.♖f1, winning.

43.♔g2! h3+!

44.♔g1!!

After 44.♔h1 h2!! White is in zugzwang, and it's a draw! Getting rid of his h-pawn will make new amazing resources available for Black: 45.♖g4 (45.♔xh2 ♕d6+ draws) 45...c4!! 46.bxc4 ♕d7 47.♖f7 ♗g6!! 48.♖f8+ ♔h7 49.♖xg6 ♕xe7 50.♖gf6, and now, thanks to the sac of the c-pawn, Black has a better square for his queen to counterattack the e3-pawn and escape with a draw!

44...h2+ 45.♔h1! ♛d7 46.♖f7!

46...♛d1+

46...♔g6 47.♖d5!!, winning.

47.♔xh2 ♛d2+ 48.♔g2 ♛d6+ 49.♔g1 ♛d1+ 50.♖f1!

No more checks, and the e-pawn eventually queens!

Affordance

The concept of affordance is taken from the field of Object Design (see *The Design of Everyday Things* by Donald Norman). It is an inherent quality of the object that attracts the user to use it in the appropriate way. The simplest example is a button which causes everyone to press it or a sofa that calls you to lay down on it. Some of these behaviours are natural and some are acquired or learned. Chess players usually learn chess affordances at an early stage – the rooks are attracted to the seventh or second rank almost by gravity, squares d5/f5 attract the white knights to occupy them, and the possibility of an attack on the king urges us to move forward with all our might.

However, affordance may become a blind spot, because players are inclined not to check other options

Affordance is an inherent quality of an object that attracts the user to use it in an appropriate way

when an affordance move stares them in the face.

Fabiano Caruana – Ian Nepomniachtchi
St. Louis Sinquefield Cup 2019
position after 28.♛g2

In this position, sacrificing on a3 looks promising, but Nepomniachtchi went 28...♗f8, and the game ended peacefully after a few moves. Apparently, he couldn't see how to proceed with the attack after:

28...♖xa3! 29.bxa3 ♛xa3 30.f3

Now if 30...♖a8, then 31.♛b2, and Black's attacking potential is exhausted. Nevertheless, the position is winning for Black.

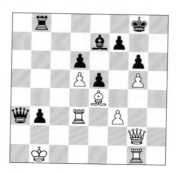

30...♛a7!!

This winning move is only three moves away from the initial position, and still very hard to see. Fortunately, the machine is a brilliant scriptwriter, specializing in creating twists in the plot all the time. Never a dull moment in its movies.

There are three compelling reasons why a human would not consider the move ♛a3-a7: First, the queen is moving away from the white king; Second, it is going backwards; and Third, it returns to the same square it

occupied two moves earlier (switch-back). It is extremely difficult for a human player to overcome all these barriers, even one by one.

Now the main threat is ...b2, and the white queen is tied up to the defence of ♖g1. White is lost.

31.♖d2 Self-blocking the white queen on the 2nd rank.

31...♖a8! And wins.

Prophylaxis while attacking

Grandmaster Arthur Kogan (with whom I share a YouTube channel on the subject) has compared a chess player in the middle of a vicious attack to a hungry animal. The animal is filled with adrenalin, trying to satisfy its primary needs urgently and possibly losing its composure and patience. This is a very dangerous moment, because the prey may hit back or escape. Psychologically speaking, one of the most difficult things to do while attacking is to hold the horses within us and briefly slow them down, if necessary. It requires us to control our id – the wild, aggressive animal inside us.

The machine is free of such biases and can change the rhythm of the game at any point. It is an excellent tool for sharpening our sense of danger when we are attacking, and for helping us to control our urges.

John William Schulten – Paul Morphy
New York 1857
position after 18.♗xc6

Here Morphy, who strives for constant harmony among his attacking forces, played **18...♖ac8?.** Nevertheless, this move is an error, throwing away the win. What can be wrong with such a nice-looking move?

The machine advises: 18...♖ec8!!. Why is it better for Black to have his rook on a8 than on e8? We have to dig deeper into this position.

White could have played **19.♔b2!** In the game White lost quickly after 19.♔d2?? ♖xc6 20.dxc6 ♗xe2 21.♖xe2 ♕xd4+ 22.♔e1 ♕g1+ 23.♔d2 ♖d8+ 24.♔c3 ♕c5+ 25.♔b2 ♘a4+!.

19...♖xc6 20.dxc6 ♗xe2

Now White's queen is actually not under attack because of Black's back rank problem, but White's main problem is still: how to get out of deadly threats like ...♘a4+ or ...♘c4+. Let's see what won't work:
21.♖xe2 ♘a4+ 22.bxa4 ♕b4, mate.
21.♕d2 ♘c4+ 22.bxc4 ♖b8+ 23.♔c3 ♕b4, mate.
21.♗d2 ♘c4+ 22.♔b1 ♕xd4, and Black wins.

But now comes the real brilliancy of the machine: **21.♖b1!!** A rare 'castling' pattern – evacuating square a1 for the king, where it can finally find relief after a long and dangerous walk.

Even the great Paul Morphy sometimes had trouble choosing the right rook.

Of course, the adventures haven't ended yet, but a human might stop his calculation here with the conclusion that he is still alive and kicking. Let's take a short trip through the amazing continuation:
21...♘a4+ 22.♔a1 ♘c3 23.♕d2 ♕xc6

24.d5!!
The only saving move, using the pin on the e-file and protecting f3! The d-pawn is like a basketball player who

takes responsibility with the last shot in the final crucial seconds.
24...♕c8 25.♖b2

Now, with the aid of the d-pawn, White has compensation for his misplaced pieces. For the engine this position is a clear 0.00!!!

■ ■ ■

Can humans play like an engine? After finding more than a thousand examples of moves missed by humans and pointed out by engines, one might think that the answer is a definite and comprehensive 'no'. However, I believe that the limits of human imagination can be significantly widened by studying hidden engine ideas that challenge common chess thinking but are within human calculating power. As mentioned above, in the computer era we meet the exceptions everywhere, so they will inevitably become part of our new patterns. ■

This article was inspired by the book that Noam Manella wrote together with Zeev Zohar, Think Like a Machine *(Quality Chess 2020). Except for the first fragment, which featured in the book, all examples presented here are new.*

The limits of human imagination can be significantly reduced by studying hidden engine ideas that are within human calculating power

Levon Aronian:

'I look forward to starting a new life'

Armenian star spurned by country's leadership switches to Team USA

The news of Levon Aronian's switch to the United States not only revealed his discontent about the situation in his country; it also showed that a year after the tragic death of his wife Arianne, he is ready to make a fresh start. In a frank interview, the world's number 5 speaks to **DIRK JAN TEN GEUZENDAM** about his darkest hours and the spiritual strength and the light of a new love that helped him back on his feet again.

When Levon Aronian appears on screen for our Skype talk, he is wearing an eye-catching orange T-shirt. It was designed by his new girlfriend Ani and shows two memes of his pet dog Ponchik. There's a dismissive Ponchik with averted eyes ('Getting no treats') and a contented thumbs-up Ponchik ('Tummy rubs for everyone'). Aronian's followers on Twitter and Facebook know that Ponchik, a white furry dog with coal-black eyes and sharp, pointed teeth, has been his loyal companion in the online tournaments during lockdown. And that he has even been a wise counsellor at crucial moments ('We had a long talk. Ponchik said this type of play is not good enough. I was given a warning'). When Aronian wants a carefree tone or a spell of comic relief, there is always Ponchik to turn to.

What he wears has often been a way to express his mood or inspiration of the moment for the Armenian. Several times he arrived for key contests dressed to the nines, as if to mark the weight and importance of the occasion. He'd show up in a striking new suit with a conspicuous tie, or with an accessory that would unavoidably draw attention. Which other chess player would wear 'Al Capone' dress shoes or a classic Borsalino fedora hat just because he felt like it?

But just as easily as he dresses up, Aronian dresses down. When he's not playing, he may go for a sports shirt with the name and number of a favourite football player or, as he does now, a playful T-shirt. A shirt that seems to send a signal. The year gone by was horrible, filled with mourning and sorrow, but he wants to embrace

life again, and his colourful shirt is matched by the upbeat 'Hi! How are you?', which are his first words.

The darkest cloud over the past year was the tragic death of his wife Arianne in a car crash. This was the absolute nadir; but there was more adversity that shook his trust in life. The brutal six-week war between Armenia and Azerbaijan over Nagorno-Karabakh that started in September cost thousands of lives and ended in an Armenian defeat and a painful peace treaty. The eruption of violence and the fate of his country heavily affected him and further undermined his trust in the current government. Gone are the days that the chess-loving president Serzh Sargsyan warmly supported the national team as they won three Olympiads, even taking

Levon Aronian together with Ponchik and his new girlfriend Ani. 'After finding a person that is very special and very deep, I could feel that I could be back.'

them home on the presidential plane. The new president, his opponent and namesake Armen Sargsyan, has mainly shown indifference. In the end, his lack of interest in chess and chess players was such that 38-year-old Aronian took a drastic decision. In early March, he announced that he was going to play for Team USA and move to St. Louis, now the American capital of chess thanks to benefactor Rex Sinquefield. Switching federations is a momentous decision for any player, but it's simply sensational if it concerns the number five player in the world who brought his native country so much glory. That is not a decision you take lightly. How did he reach that point?

'We have seen big changes in Armenia. From the first day that the new government came into power in 2018, I could feel that they were trying to make it clear that our chess achievements had nothing to do with the previous government. I could feel that in the press and also in the street. In a small country like Armenia, a lot of things are controlled, and they are easily controlled. The way you are perceived, even by common people, can be modulated by the government. I could feel that the way people were sending me messages or talking to me was kind of disrespectful. And all those changes were solely motivated by the wish to do everything different from the previous government. Let's do it the other way, let's fire everybody who was working under the previous government.

Everything that had been achieved by the previous government was being undone. I don't look at change as something negative, but there's change and there's let's destroy everything and build everything anew, as under the communist slogan. I felt we were going in that direction, just destroying everything to begin with. Then I met with a couple of officials, and I could tell that they were not interested in what I had to say. I felt that I was just being mocked, and I respect myself too much for that.

'Our former president, Serzh Sargsyan, is also the head of the chess federation. He's a decent chess player. There were some meetings and they said, he has to go. Some young guy who had nothing to do with chess came and said he was going to replace him. To which we as chess players just said, no, it's not going to happen. If he's going to go, it's us who will decide who is going to replace him. He is not in chess because of political gain, we know that for sure. He was always there at the chess club, always supporting us. Even if he is not in power anymore, it's disrespectful to remove a guy who helped us to achieve our successes and be Olympiad champions. He said, I don't mind leaving, but we didn't want to have it, and he is still the president of the federation.

'The people who were supposed to replace him, they know nothing about chess and I wouldn't say they're very sympathetic people. For example, immediately when they came to power, they said, we are not going to sponsor the chess school anymore, because grandmasters are not supposed to get so much money. They are getting something like 900 dollars a month, they will work for 100 dollars from now on. The grandmasters refused, so the school was closed. This is the attitude. They are not chess players. For them a grandmaster is just a guy who got a title without much work.'

All this feels strange, with the long chess tradition there is in Armenia. Your successes and the successes of the national team were always a moment of national pride.
'Yes, and for me personally, there is no bigger joy than living in my country and speaking my language and being in the city where I was born. But I want to continue playing chess, I want to continue dedicating myself to chess. At some point, it just got too toxic. What I did was basically very painful to myself, but I had to do it, because being disrespected made me feel as if I couldn't really concentrate on chess. I took a decision, and I am of course very grateful to the American side, to Rex and his team, that they

didn't question my motives and didn't say no to my request.'

You say that the situation got toxic, that people were manipulated against you. At the same time, there must have been people who sided with you.
'Yes, a lot of people, intellectuals who understand that it's not easy to be a chess player. It requires dedication. At the same time, a lot of other people say this is a stupid job, we don't need chess players in Armenia, it's not necessary for the country to succeed, it's better for us to spend this money in other fields. Which, of course, is a possible choice; it's not as if I am bitter about anything. Every country makes its choice about the way it wants to develop. It's just that I have dedicated my life to chess and I want to continue dedicating my life to chess. And if my country says, you don't deserve to have any funding and this school has to be closed, I understand that this is the attitude of this government, and I move on – and continue doing what I am doing, because nothing can stop me from working on chess. That's part of me.'

You are going to join Team USA, with the support of Rex Sinquefield. Are you planning to move to St. Louis?
'Yes, I am going to live in St. Louis, and I have great respect for Rex. People who think that he is a guy who buys players and takes them away from their country don't really know him as a person. I have never seen this attitude. He's a patriot of his city. He wants St. Louis to blossom in chess, and I love what he is doing. And I am happy to join that company of Leinier (Dominguez), Fabi (Caruana) and other grandmasters. These are my friends, people that I play tennis with during tournaments.'

You specifically mentioned Fabiano Caruana as someone supporting your move...
'He's a good friend of mine and we got much closer a year ago. He supported

Levon Aronian during the Skype conversation, happily offering a better view of the orange T-shirt with the Ponchik memes.

'I am welcoming the opportunity to become an American citizen, but ethnically and culturally I am still Armenian'

me with his kind words and actions. I respect that. His general attitude. We're competitors, we're supposed to hate each other (laughs), and somebody is being very supportive and nice. I value that. You know, generally, despite of me being a fighter, last year was very difficult. And I look forward to starting a new life.'

I got the feeling that when six years ago you returned to Armenia to live there, it seemed like part of a trend of more successful Armenians returning home from abroad.
'Yes, I felt that I'd achieved a lot, and I wanted to go back to my country and give back. To live here, work here, support other players. Just by being in your country, especially if it's a small and poor country, you are kind of supporting the general public. That was what I wanted to do – come back and be useful. And I could tell that wherever I could be of any help, I was asked for advice and I was treated with the respect that I felt I deserved. And when that is gone and you're being ignored, you kind of feel that maybe it's not the right time to be here. Because eventually, maybe in twenty years, I will be back. I don't know, I cannot plan what's going to happen with my life. I am welcoming the opportunity to become an American citizen and play for the United States. But ethnically and culturally I am still Armenian.'

Is there an Armenian community in St. Louis?
'There is a church in Granite City, not far from St. Louis. There is a little community, mostly students that were in Washington University and stayed there. But there's the chess players! We have two, I think even three Akobians. There's Varuzhan Akobian, and I think Vladimir (Akopian's) son is studying there. And also we have

Aram Hakobyan, a young and good player.'

As you mentioned, last year was a terribly difficult year for you. There was the tragic death of your wife Arianne. How did you survive the next months, what kept you going?
'I wouldn't say that I am a religious man, but I believe that there are things that we can't really prevent, no matter how hard you try. And I had plans with Arianne, and that was what was keeping me going. Knowing that I should live and that I should fight, and I should just be what I am. Of course there are our memories, and she's a part of me, and therefore I continue. She always wanted to see me play chess, and that's what I am dedicated to.'

You're a great lover of music. Sometimes music can console, sometimes it cannot. Did you manage to find any consolation or help in music?
'Of course. The amount of classical music I listened to when I was mourning was tremendous. And Bach always comes to the rescue, of course. He's there at any moment, on any occasion. More than anything else, I listened to his works for violin, for piano, for solo instruments. They are closer to me than his oratorios.'

For several months you disappeared from public life. Then you returned to play chess. Was that just an attempt, or were you convinced that it would help you?
'I had to do it, because I was feeling sick, just physically sick from not doing anything. And I knew that I was not going to play well. I knew that it wouldn't be a success, mildly speaking, but I knew I had to do it. Then I slowly got into the rhythm, and then I met Ani, and then I got

back on my feet again. I felt that she understood, that she was feeling my mourning and was mourning with me and helping me to come out of this situation. There was a very spiritual connection. I met her through friends here in Yerevan, and she wanted to be just a friend. She was not interested in anything else. First we met as friends and after that I understood that she was somebody that I wanted to see in my life. I wanted to see her every day. We have a lot in common, and then she also felt that I was that person. Yeah, I think that after finding a person that is very special and very deep, I could feel that I could be back.'

Many people were happy for you, but as happens on social media, you also got attacked. Was that something that hurt you?
'No, it didn't. You can't expect people to understand such tragedy, because very few people will get to experience it. Going through the tragedy of a young person you love dying, with you sharing so much with that young person, and seeing all of this getting lost. I don't expect many people to understand it. And then, when you experience something like that, you are in such a state that you want something deep and something spiritual in your life. Something bigger. And then I got it. It was not as if I said to myself, I've got to do this and that, this is the plan of recovery or... Because people on the side-line may think, oh he looked at the time, he looked at the clock, and said, I want to do that. I never in my life went and had a relationship just out of the air or ever had a desire for something that is shallow.'

Regarding the spiritual side, I saw somewhere that your mother told you that the blows that you get from fate are administered according to what you can take. That expressed great trust in you.
'It's a saying we have in Armenia, that God sends challenges according to

'It's a saying we have in Armenia, that God sends challenges according to the size of the person's heart'

the size of the person's heart. I know that I have always been true in my life, and I've always been honest to myself and to others. Therefore the challenges that come, I should just accept them, you know. Because all of us have done wrong, but I have never seen myself betray anybody, or betray myself. Therefore it's a challenge. I don't look at it as a punishment. Although I am not religious in that sense, and don't belong to any religion, I am part of Christian culture where everybody feels that they should admit that they're guilty, that this is a punishment. But in my case I don't see that I've done something wrong in my life or hurt anybody or been jealous of anybody. That's what my mom probably meant. That this is a challenge, and it's a challenge that you have to accept and respect and you have to try to fight the adversity.'

One of the things we've often discussed is your immense hunger, particularly for cultural experiences. Could this wish to deal with this challenge be in some way in line with this trait in your character?
'Yeah, of course. I am a stubborn person, and I've had many bad things happening to me, even in my career;

bad play, or I've been betrayed by my friends. But I am happy I am never bitter or upset or angry with anybody. It's not part of me. If I am disappointed in you or anyone else, I just leave. I don't feel any anger towards you, and I work on myself. That's what I believe in, and that's what I do. I work to be better.'

Last October you returned to over-the-board chess in Stavanger, in Norway Chess. You played really well, but at the same time there was the war between Armenia and Azerbaijan over Nagorno-Karabakh that affected you a lot. Do you think it hit you extra hard because of the situation you were already in?
'Yeah, it affected me because I was trying so hard to help my country, to do everything I could. We saw things that were just terrible and the government was telling us completely different things. We were told that we were fighting very hard, and I knew and am proud of people who were there fighting, but I also know that there was a strange kind of optimism

and a strange kind of information that was untrue. That disappointed not just me, but also a lot of other people, because we didn't know what was really happening.'

Did you feel betrayed by the concessions that the government made in the peace treaty that was brokered?
'I mean, you can lose; there is nothing wrong about losing. You're not strong, so it's normal that you might lose. Then you need to work harder. But you can lose without the need of sacrificing everything. We lost more than five thousand young guys. That is heart-breaking. This did not happen in a way that I saw as justified. I myself, if the time comes, I will go and I don't mind fighting to protect my people. I'm not a pacifist. I believe the same things that my grandparents believed in when they were fighting against Nazi-Germany. They fought and they were ready to sacrifice their lives for the freedom of their nation. Of course, there's nothing beautiful about war but it has to be done at times. And I am a

person who believes that it has to be done. But when we get to know that some young guys who had no idea what was going on, who didn't know how to shoot, that they were sent into the war... That is heart-breaking, because we know that a human life is very valuable.'

Both Armenia and Azerbaijan are strong chess nations, and leading players expressed their feelings on social media. Was it difficult then and afterwards to play against Azeri players, whom in fact you know so well?
'Look, in my life, never for one second did I feel that Azeri, Turks, or whatever nation was my personal enemy. I never expressed such beliefs. I remember reading a book by Elie Wiesel, and his message about the Holocaust was that the tragedy was not that these were Germans or a nation doing something to other nations, but that these are humans doing things to humans. What was heart-breaking for me was that there were mercenaries, it was very ugly, there was forbidden weaponry, and all these things were happening to my country. But I will never be a tool for any national propaganda. Never in any message did I ever say anything that was not part of me. And it was disappointing for me that some of my colleagues from Azerbaijan were using very aggressive language. But I don't mind, I'm just playing chess. Maybe I was friends with some of them before, maybe I won't be friends with them anymore, most likely, but it doesn't change my respect for them as competitors and chess players, great chess players.'

In Norway Chess you beat Magnus in the final round and without the Armageddon games you would have shared first with Carlsen and Firouzja. Did that do you a lot of good?
'Yeah, of course, it's a relief. You know that you can still beat strong players, you feel that you haven't lost

Three days after he won the 2017 World Cup in Tbilisi, Levon Aronian married Arianne Caoili in the presence of Armenia's president Serzh Sargsyan (who acted as the couple's 'godfather') and his wife. 'I had plans with Arianne, and that was what was keeping me going. Knowing that I should live and that I should fight, and I should just be what I am.'

your touch. After a year like this it was very important.'

How do you look at your chess now? What are your plans, what are you going to do in St. Louis? What are your ambitions?
'Well, my ambitions are always the same, but in St. Louis I will have a chess atmosphere. I just want to be in a chess atmosphere, work on chess and see where it will take me. I started blossoming late, I was a late bloomer. I got all my desires, and my spirits are high. I just want to play and see what happens.'

There was often the feeling that the pressure that came from your compatriots, or from yourself because you knew their expectations, that this didn't help. Is this something that might be less now?
'Yeah, maybe. Maybe, I don't really know. Most expectations come from myself (smiles).'

What are you telling yourself?
'I am telling myself that I am a hell of a player (laughs). So I just need

to work on it. I need to work on my craft.'

And you have the hunger for that?
'Yes, more than ever.'

There is this assumption that when you reach a certain age in chess, this hunger decreases, but you feel it's still there.
'Oh, of course things become harder, the older you get. You can't say, oh, I understand the game much better... You do understand the game much better, but you play much worse! (laughs). Because you basically don't have the same energy. But! For the moment I feel very energetic, and I just want to see what happens. I am curious. You know, it's a golden era of chess. A lot of people are playing, there is a lot of interest, and I am not going to let this era go without me in it.'

And you should show some people your place in the historical hierarchy. I must say I was pretty shocked to see you in 33rd place in the 50 greatest players of all time. Of course, it was an impossible task that Jan Gustafsson and Peter Heine Nielsen set themselves, but still...

'Well, I spoke about it with Fabi actually, and my view is that if I am not in the top 20, then there is something wrong. I should definitely be there. But that's the thing with people when they look at modern chess players or basketball players. For instance, take Magnus. He is definitely the greatest of all time, but he is playing now. Or LeBron James, he is the greatest of all time, but people perceive it like no, no, of course not, let's find somebody else from a different era.'

You might look at it statistically and say this or that player had better results. But putting Zukertort ahead of you, what's this?

'Well, this was the era when they couldn't tell a bishop from a knight. I am kidding, of course. They were decent Candidate-Master-level players.'

Now suppose he won twenty tournaments, but he didn't.

'Well, he probably won a lot of games playing for stakes (laughs). But I also did that! Just people don't know about it. As a young player, I used to play for stakes during the Linares Opens, in the evenings, to make a living. Playing blitz till 3 am many times, at first for a hundred pesetas, then 500 pesetas a game. These games should be part of my history and maybe my ranking will go up (with a mischievous smile). I actually made a friend like that. Alex Wohl. I was playing for stakes and Alex was suggesting moves for my opponent. And I got really angry. And then he said, it's just a hundred pesetas. And I said, a hundred pesetas is big money for me. And he opened his wallet and offered me to take all the money he had. And I didn't, and then I made a friend.'

Talking about friends, we can't have this talk without speaking about

Ponchik. What role does Ponchik play in your everyday life?

'He's a great inspiration, a friend, an assistant. I love how inspiring it is to have a dog in my life. I am very happy that people like him, and I want to share him with the whole world.'

I am not an expert, but is he a particular kind of breed?

'No, no, he is a stray dog. Just like me (laughs).'

And he is also full of life and curiosity and hunger...

'Yes, full of hunger for sure! Guaranteed.'

■ ■ ■

Creative and fighting

Levon Aronian played the following game in the Preliminaries of the Magnus Carlsen Invitational. With a forceful exchange sacrifice he gets such pressure on Sergey Karjakin's position that the Russian 'Minister of Defence' collapses.

NOTES BY
Levon Aronian

Levon Aronian
Sergey Karjakin
Magnus Carlsen Invitational
2021 (prelim 3)
Queen's Pawn Game, London System

1.d4 ♘f6 2.♘f3 d5 3.♗f4

The Grischuk System, which used to be called the London.

The Grischuk System, which used to be called the London

3...♗f5 Every time I see the ♗f4/...♗f5 symmetry I am amused! In so many positions Black can allow ♕b3 without any bad consequences.
4.c4 e6 5.♕b3
I had looked at this line with my second Manuel Petrosyan, and we came to the conclusion that it's slightly more comfortable for White.
5...♘c6 Both 5...dxc4 and 5...♘bd7 are possible and very solid. The game move is not great, but it leads to a mess. Useful in a rapid game!
6.♘bd2
I remembered that 6.c5 is more principled, but I wanted to play solidly.
6...♘a5
This was a surprise. I had mainly looked at 6...♗d6 or 6...♗e7. The text-move is very much in the spirit of ...♘c6, but for some reason I did not pay much attention to it while preparing.
7.♕a4+ c6

8.cxd5 A second-rate move. I saw that 8.c5 was the best move, but since Sergey was playing fast, I wanted to confuse him. After 8.c5 b5 9.♕a3 and b3, White keeps a nice grip, since it will take a long time for the a5-knight to become an active participant in the game.
8...b5 Here 8...exd5, with the idea of ...♕b6, was even stronger.
9.♕d1 exd5
9...cxd5 is bad in view of 10.e4, with big problems for the black king.
10.g3

I was happy with this move. At least now the position looks unusual.

10...♘c4 11.b3 ♘xd2 12.♗xd2

12...♗e4 A strange mistake that makes my sloppy 8.cxd5 work nicely. After 12...♗a3 13.♗g2 0-0 14.♘h4 ♗e4 Black is seriously better due to the dominating bishop on a3, just like my h3-bishop! I think my opponent had forgotten about the possibility of the exchange sac.

13.♗h3

Both 13.♕c1 and 13.a4 also refute 12...♗e4, but I already saw my knight on c6!

13...♗a3 14.0-0 0-0 15.♘e5 ♗b2

15...♖e8 is mathematically better, but still won't equalize, even after 16.♗c1.

16.♘xc6 ♕b6 17.♖c1

Levon Aronian: 'It's a golden era in chess. I am not letting this era go without me in it.'

LENNART OOTES

White dominates because of the e4-bishop being completely out of play.

17...♗xc1 18.♕xc1 ♖fe8 19.♗a5

A mistake that went unpunished. Protecting the e2-pawn with 19.♖e1 was the accurate way to secure a large advantage.

19...♕b7

Instead, 19...♕a6 would have created strong counterplay that could lead to equality. Sergey and I had missed that Black has a threat in ...♗b1, attacking both the e2-pawn and the a2-pawn.

20.f3 ♗g6 Here 20...♗b1 makes no sense, since after 21.♘e5 Black can't do any damage.

21.♘e5

21...b4 More stubborn was 21...♔h8, with the idea of ...♘g8/...f6. The text-move only makes the b-pawn weaker.

22.♕d2 ♖ab8 23.♖c1

The rest does not require any comment. Black is slowly losing material due to his passive pieces.

23...h6 24.♘c6 ♖a8 25.♗xb4 ♘d7 26.♘a5 ♕a6 27.♗xd7 ♖xe2 28.♖c6 ♖xd2 29.♖xa6 ♖xa2 30.♖d6 ♔h7 31.♖xd5 ♖b8 32.♖b5 ♖a1+ 33.♔f2 ♖a2+ 34.♔e3

Black resigned. ∎

Blitz with Walter

Walter Shawn Browne, the terror of US tournaments in the 70's and early 80's, was also the catalyst behind creating interest in blitz in the US and an indefatigable proponent of separate ratings for blitz and tournament chess. After winning the US Championship six times – the last time in 1983, Walter's results in tournaments began to deteriorate, probably because of his new-found love – poker. He immediately adapted to the new reality. His strength in blitz was on a par with the best blitz chess players in the world and by promoting blitz, he would give himself decades of chess longevity.

I first met Walter, along with many of the national top players, at my first Closed US Championship in 1984. I started with a score of 4½/5, including a win over Walter, when he misplayed a system in the Classical Queen's Indian, which then became the regular battleground for our games in both tournaments and blitz. Whenever we had a difference of opinion in a position that occurred in our tournament games, we would place bets on those positions and play out a series of blitz games to decide who was right. He loved betting, and I remember him betting on a series of results in different tournaments where he was only a spectator.

It was fun being around Walter, because he always had an original opinion to share, and when I had dinner with him at the fateful 2015 National Open, just a few days before

It isn't that long ago that blitz was frowned upon as a frivolous exercise that might well do damage to your 'real game'. But there were pioneers. **MAXIM DLUGY** pays tribute to Walter Browne, six-time US champion, founder of the World Blitz Chess Association and editor of *Blitz Chess*, the one and only magazine ever totally dedicated to his passion.

his untimely passing, I had no idea this was the last time I would enjoy his company.

In 1988, Walter Browne formed the World Blitz Chess Association to promote blitz – by rating all blitz tournaments he could get his hands on and publishing them every three months in his self-published magazine *Blitz Chess*. For a $12 fee, members of his association, which some jokingly called the Walter Browne Chess Association, would get three magazines packed with analysis by Walter Browne and some great contributors, as well as get their ratings published in the back of the magazine. Grandmasters were exempt from paying the fees, of course, and this allowed Walter to rate many of the best players in the world, including Kasparov, Karpov, Tal, Kortchnoi, Yusupov and even yours truly.

When I started my ascent in the chess world, blitz was a big part of my life, and by winning the US Open Blitz Championship with an overall score of 28½-½, I managed to squeeze past Garry Kasparov to become the highest-rated blitz player, four points ahead of the World Champion with a blitz rating of 2777, in the December 1991 issue of *Blitz Chess*. Since I had already retired from professional chess, having started my career in finance, this was a very nice aside to my mainstream life, all courtesy of Walter Browne's intense involvement in the promotion of blitz.

To show his involvement in a deeper way, I will showcase some of his games, with stories surrounding them. In this way, hopefully, we will all remember this great pioneer of blitz and the legacy he left us.

I will start with what Walter called 'one of the sharpest blitz games he has ever played', against the Magician from Riga, World Champion Mikhail Tal. It was played at the 1991 Pan-Pacific Blitz Championships. Tal was visiting San Francisco to participate in the Pan-Pacific Grandmaster tournament, won by Eugenio Torre. Even though the blitz tournament boasted a meagre first prize of $200, and the players had to play a total of 23 games, Tal, who (unlike the other players) had no free days (he had to make up for two missed games in the GM event due to his late arrival), could not refuse a blitz competition! I include Walter's notes to the game, along with my comments in brackets.

Walter Browne
Mikhail Tal
San Francisco 1991
Slav Defence

1.d4 d5 2.c4 c6 3.♘c3 e5

Down at the 1985 Taxco Interzonal, Tal agreed to a blitz match, in which he overwhelmed me with many sharp and unusual sacrificial openings. I knew that 4.cxd5 cxd5 5.♘f3 e4 6.♘e5 was currently popular, but I wanted to create something. At the very least, I thought I'd surprise him too!

4.cxd5 cxd5 5.e4 dxe4
5...exd4?! 6.♘xd5 (6.♕xd4 also gives White a big edge – MD) 6...♘c6 7.♗b5 ♗c5 8.♘f3 is better for White.

A legend in many ways, Walter Browne was ahead of his time in his fight to get blitz recognized as chess that mattered.

6.♗b5+ 6.dxe5? ♕xd1+ is duck soup for Tal. (An amazing comment from Walter!! Does anyone know what he means ☺ – MD.)
6... ♗d7 6...♘d7? 7.dxe5, with a winning position, since e6 is in the air.
7.dxe5 7.♕b3 exd4 8.♗c4 dxc3?

(8...♘f6! is extremely strong, preserving all the advantages of a huge centre. After 9.♗xf7+ ♔e7 10.♘ge2 ♘a6! 11.♘d5+ ♔xf7 12.♘c7+ ♔g6 13.♘f4+ ♔f5 14.♕h3+ ♘g4 15.♕xa6 ♔f6 Black wins! – MD) 9.♗xf7+ ♔e7 10.♗xg8, winning.

7...♘c6
True to his nature, Tal keeps the tension. I needed to win this final game, however, and I was worried I mightn't have much after 7...♗xb5

By promoting blitz, Walter Browne would give himself decades of chess longevity

8.♕xd8+ ♔xd8 9.♘xb5, when after 9...♗b4+ 10.♗d2 ♗xd2+ 11.♔xd2 ♘c6 12.f4 exf3 13.♘xf3 ♔e7 Black seems to be OK.

8.♕d5! ♕e7 At the time I thought 8...♘b4 was best, although 9.♕xe4 (sometime during a restless night, and while I slept, I analysed 9.e6!?

ANALYSIS DIAGRAM

9...♘xd5 (9...fxe6! is the only way to equality. After 10.♕xe6+ ♗e7 11.♗xd7+ ♕xd7 12.♕xd7+ ♔xd7 13.♔e2 the position is equal – MD) 10.♗xd7+ ♔e7 11.♘xd5+ ♔d6 12.♗f4+ ♔xd5) 9...♗xb5 10.♘xb5 ♖c8?? 11.♘d6+ ♗xd6 12.exd6+ wins. (In fact, 9.♕xb7! leads to a decisive advantage – MD.)

9.♗f4 (It's strange that Walter didn't consider the natural 9.♘xe4 or 9.♘ge2, which look quite promising – MD.)

9...g5?! 9...f5 10.0-0-0 0-0-0 11.♗c4 was Tal's reason not to play 9...f5, although here, after 11...g5 12.♗e3 f4, Black is close to winning. It's simpler to play 11.♕c4!, with a large advantage. (9...f6!, undermining the e-pawn, was the strongest, when Black has excellent chances for a balanced game. But that wouldn't be Tal – MD.)

10.♗g3? (10.♗e3, not mentioned by Walter, would have been extremely strong. Black can't win back the e-pawn, because then White wins with 10...♕xe5 11.♗xc6, so he would lose the e-pawn, with a very bad game – MD.)

10...♗g7 (10...a6 11.♗a4 f5! was the correct way for Black to get to counterplay, with a complicated but balanced game – MD.)

11.♕xe4

11...♘xe5?
This should have lost quickly.

12.♘d5 (12.♗xe5 ♕xe5 13.♗xd7+ ♔xd7 14.0-0-0+ ♔c8 15.♕d3 was simply winning – MD.)

12...f5
12...♕d6 13.♘f3 ♗xb5 14.♘xe5 0-0-0 15.♖c1+ ♔b8 16.♘d7+, and crunch. (True but strange, Mikhail didn't reach out to the stars with a queen sacrifice. After 12...♗xb5! 13.♘xe7 ♘d3+ 14.♔d2 ♘xe7 15.♗d6 0-0 16.♗xe7 ♖fe8 White is far better, but would Walter have been up to the job in that case? – MD.)

13.♕e2!

13...♕d6 13...♗xb5 14.♕xb5+ ♕d7 15.♘c7+, winning.

14.♘f3

14...f4 14...♕xd5 15.♗xd7+ ♕xd7 16.♘xe5 ♕e7 17.0-0-0, with a raging attack, because White wins after 17...♘f6 18.♕b5+ ♔f8 19.♘d7+ ♘xd7 20.♗d6.

15.♘xf4??

15...gxf4??
(Both players, and even Walter in the comments, missed the intermediate shot 15...♕b4+!!, which would have won on the spot for Black – MD.)

16.♗xd7+

16...♔xd7?
(An amazing move by Tal. After the correct 16...♔f8 17.0-0 ♘xf3+ 18.♕xf3 ♕xd7 19.♖fd1 ♕f7 20.♗xf4 ♘f6 White would certainly have had

more than ample compensation for the piece, but in a blitz game anyone can win – MD.)

17.♖d1 ♘xf3+ 18.♕xf3 ♖e8+ 19.♔f1 ♗d4 20.♗xf4 ♕a6+ 21.♔g1 ♘e7 22.♖xd4+

And Black overstepped in a hopeless position.

The following game is from a blitz tournament in 'The Land of the Sky', Ashville, North Carolina. Walter Browne shows his teeth against 'Dzindzi', Roman Dzindzichashvili, who in those days was one of the best blitz players in the world. They split their match and beat up the other players, scoring 9/10 each, and splitting the first two prizes. Here's Walter's win over Roman with the white pieces, which – as he made sure to point out in an extra bit of information – was played in the morning. Again the notes are based on Walter's, with a couple of asides from me.

Walter Browne
Roman Dzindzichashvili
Los Angeles 1991
Queen's Gambit Declined

1.d4 d5 2.c4 ♗f5

(Roman loved to play this sub-line, which I think has to be refuted with 3.♕b3! – MD.)

3.cxd5 ♗xb1 4.♕a4+ c6 5.dxc6
5.♖xb1 ♕xd5 6.♘f3 ♘f6 7.e3 b5 8.♕a5, and White is clearly better.
5...♘xc6 6.♖xb1 ♕xd4 7.♕xd4 ♘xd4

I needed to win this second of two games. That explains Dzindzi's choice; but he hasn't equalized yet.

8.e3 ♘c6 No good is 8...♘c2+? 9.♔d1 ♘b4 10.♗d2 ♘c6 11.♘f3 e5 12.♗b5, with a pleasant advantage for White.
9.♘f3 e6

10.♗d2?! 10.♗b5 ♗b4+ 11.♔e2 ♘e7 12.a3 ♗d6 13.♖d1 0-0-0 14.♘g5 sets Black a real dilemma, since 14...♘e5 would allow 15.f4!.
10...♗b4

11.♗b5?! As I said, it was very early. Clearly better was 11.♗xb4! ♘xb4 12.♗b5+ ♔e7 13.a3? (13.♖c1!, taking over the c-file, really does give White a huge advantage – MD.) 13...♘d5 14.e4 ♘c7 15.♗d3 ♘f6 16.♔e2

and White's edge is based on the poor placement of Black's knight on c7. (Not sure if I agree. I think the symmetrical

pawn structure and the somewhat blocked light-squared bishops give the knights equality after, say, 16...♘d7 – MD.)

11...♗xd2+ 12.♔xd2 ♖c8 13.♔e2 ♘e7 14.♖hc1 0-0 15.♘g5! h6 16.♘e4 ♖fd8 17.♘c5 b6 18.♘a6 ♘e5 19.♘c7!

I am threatening 20.♗a6, taking over the c-file.

19...♘d5! (Dzindzi reacts quickly, as he must. In fact, this is a serious mistake. Black had many reasonable moves that would have kept the balance, e.g. 19...♘5c6! 20.♘a6 ♘e5, with equality – MD.)
20.♘a6? 20.♘xd5! ♖xc1 21.♖xc1 ♖xd5 22.♖c8+ ♔h7 23.a4, with the idea of ♖c7, looks unpleasant for Black. (I would simply add that this is the kind of unpleasant where resigning becomes a reasonable idea. E.g.: 23...g5 24.♖c7 a5 25.f4 gxf4 26.exf4 ♘g6 27.♖xf7+ ♔g8 28.♖b7 ♘xf4+ 29.♔f3, with a winning endgame – MD.)
20...♘e7 21.b4?

White wins after 21.f4 ♘d7 22.♖xc8 ♘xc8 23.♖d1. (While this is true, 21...♘g4! keeps the balance – MD.)

21...♘d7??

21...♘d5 would have ruined my morning. (Walter is absolutely correct. White would have had no defence against the family fork on c3. Instead he plays a losing move – MD.)

22.♘c7?

The simple 22.♖xc8 ♘xc8 23.♖d1 would have finished the game.

22...♘c5 23.♘a6?

The comedy of errors continues. White should trade knights, then on b6 and work the weak b6-pawn.

23...♘xa6? (Here 23...♘e4! would have won again – MD.)

24.♗xa6 ♖xc1 25.♖xc1 ♖d7 26.e4

26...f6 26...♖d4 27.♖c7 ♔f8 is equal. (Actually, after 28.a3 ♖xe4+ 29.♔d3 White still has something to play for – MD.)

27.♔e3 ♔f7 28.♗b5 ♖b7 29.♗a6 ♖d7 30.a4 g5 31.g3 h5 32.f4 h4?! (Black is close to equality if he can create outposts for his knight. After 32...gxf4+ 33.gxf4 f5! 34.♗b5 ♖b7 the position is equal – MD.)

33.♗c4?! (33.fxg5 fxg5 34.♗b5 ♖d6 35.♗c7 a5 36.bxa5 bxa5 37.♖c5 hxg3 38.hxg3, and Black has a tough defensive job ahead – MD.)

At the 2014 Reykjavik Open. Walter Browne remained active as a chess and poker player till his death on 24 June 2015.

33...hxg3?

(33...gxf4+ 34.gxf4 f5, with equality, was the only way. Both sides had missed this obvious intermediate move – MD.)

34.hxg3?

(34.f5! simply picks up an extra pawn, with a winning position – MD.)

34...gxf4+ 35.gxf4 f5 36.e5 a5 37.bxa5 bxa5 38.♖h1 ♖c7 39.♔d4 ♘c6+ 40.♔c3 ♔g6 41.♖g1+ ♔f7 42.♖g5 ♘e7 43.♔d3 ♖b7 44.♖h5 ♔g6 45.♖h1 ♘d5 46.♗xd5 ♖d7 47.♔c4

And though Black would have held this endgame, White won on time.

An excellent demonstration of Browne's aggressive positional style can be seen in the next game against GM Gennady Zaichik from the World Open Blitz Championship 1991, which I somehow skipped. Georgi Orlov won the Championship with 10½-1½, while Joel Benjamin and Walter tied for second with 10-2. The notes are based on Walter's.

Walter Browne
Gennady Zaichik
Philadelphia 1991
Benoni Defence

1.d4 ♘f6 2.c4 e6 3.♘f3 c5 4.d5 exd5 5.cxd5 d6 6.♘c3 g6 7.e4 ♗g7 8.h3 0-0 9.♗d3

Unfortunately, Walter was ahead of his time. FIDE was reluctant to rate anything except tournament chess

9...a6 A mistake, according to modern theory. While 9...b5 is the most common way to continue in this position, 9...♖e8 and 9...♘a6 have recently found some strong followers. **10.a4 b6 11.0-0 ♘h5 12.♖e1 ♖e8 13.♗g5 ♗f6 14.♗h6!**

White wants to trade bishops on h6, preparing to defend with the queen in case of 14...♗g7. Black's knight is tragically misplaced.
14...♘d7 15.g4! Why not force this knight into instant humiliation?
15...♗g7 16.♕d2 ♘e5 17.♘xe5 ♗xe5 18.♔g2 White has methodically advanced his kingside. Black is busted.

18...♗d7 Black's last chance was to strike with ...f5 and let the chips fall where they may. After 18...f5 19.f4 ♗d4 20.♗g5 ♕d7 21.♘e2! fxg4 22.♘xd4 gxh3+ 23.♔h2 cxd4 24.♖g1 White has a positionally winning game, but playing this in a blitz game would have been quite a challenge.
19.f4 ♗d4 20.♘e2 ♕h4 21.♘xd4

♕xh6 22.♘f3 f6?!
Black's position is pretty bad, but this allows White a fast breakthrough.

23.♔g3! (It was possible to break through with 23.e5 dxe5 24.fxe5 ♕xd2+ 25.♘xd2 ♖xe5 26.♖xe5 fxe5 27.♘c4, with a winning endgame, but Walter wants to end it in the middle-game – MD.)
23...f5 24.e5 fxg4 25.hxg4 ♗xg4

A good attempt for counterplay by Zaichik, but it falls short. White's pieces coordinate well in defence.
26.♔xg4 ♖f8 27.♘g5 ♕h5+ 28.♔g3 ♕h6 29.♖h1 ♘h5+

30.♖xh5! ♕xh5 31.e6 ♕h6 32.♗e4 ♕g7 33.♖h1 h6 34.♘f7 ♖xf7 35.exf7+ ♔xf7 36.♔f3 h5 37.♖g1

And White won soon after.

By the end of 1992, Walter Browne had around a thousand rated members. Almost 40 grandmasters had received a rating thanks to his tireless efforts to rate every blitz tournament he could lay his hands on. He spent the bulk of his time editing and creating his *Blitz Chess* magazine, and helping to organize blitz tournaments all over the world, from the most remote chess location in the United States to Nepal, often donating memberships and sometimes chess clocks, whenever needed. Unfortunately, he was a little bit ahead of his time. Although everyone loved playing blitz, FIDE was reluctant to rate anything except tournament chess. When I was President of the US Chess Federation [1990-93 – ed.], I pushed for the creation of a Quick Rating System, rating events with games lasting from 10 minutes to 30 minutes. This did give some impetus to 'trusting' the idea that it's possible to rate more than just tournaments with standard time-controls. Eventually, blitz ratings were also established by the USCF, making it one of the first federations to recognize that chess players like being rated, no matter what-time control they choose. Walter and I always believed in blitz chess, and I am happy I got to spend a lot of time with him discussing these issues. ∎

MAXIMize
your Tactics
with Maxim Notkin

Find the best move in the positions below

Solutions on page 87

1. White to play

2. White to play

3. White to play

4. White to play

5. White to play

6. White to play

7. White to play

8. White to play

9. Black to play

GIBRALTAR, MAY-JUNE 2021

THE WOMEN'S

FIDE

GRAND PRIX

is coming to Gibraltar!

 HM Government of Gibraltar

 GSLA.gi

 TOTAL

Further information: www.wgp2019.fide.com
www.gibchess.com / chess@caletahotel.gi

SPONSORED BY

 Entain

 SITUS CONSTRUCTION by Grupo Confranllves

 PKF Canillas

 THE CALETA HOTEL GIBRALTAR Health, Beauty and Conference Centre

 GIB GIBRALTAR VISITGIBRALTAR.gi

GIB INVEST

Gibtelecom

 HAMMONDS PROVIDING SOLUTIONS

 GRUPO CASAIS

 IMPERIAL GROUP

 SACCONE & SPEED SINCE 1839

 BASEWELL LTD

Judit Polgar

The fruits of harmony

His career was long and rich. Vasily Smyslov conquered the chess crown when he was 36, and at the age of 62, he was a Candidate for the last time. **JUDIT POLGAR** remembers the seventh World Champion, who affectionately called her 'Tal in a skirt'.

For players from my generation, Vasily Smyslov was a grandmaster from a remote and completely different time. He had been at his peak in the 1950s, when he disputed three World Championship matches with Mikhail Botvinnik. In 1957, Smyslov won and held the title for one year.

Smyslov remained an active player for many decades and continued to be a member of the formidable Soviet Olympiad team until 1972. However, his career as a world title Candidate did not seem to last that long. In the years following his lost return match with Botvinnik, he qualified for the Candidates only twice. In 1959, he only scored an 'honourable' fourth place, five points behind the winner, Mikhail Tal. And in 1965, he lost his quarter-final match against Efim Geller by a whopping 5½-2½.

As the years passed, that match seemed to have ended Smyslov's ambitions to get to the Candidates. Time does not forgive anybody... However, 18 years later, aged 62 already, Smyslov sensationally made it to the 1983 Candidates' Final, only

to lose there to the future champion, the very young Garry Kasparov.

In modern chess, such a performance at an advanced age is unparalleled. True, connoisseurs remember Lasker's third place at the 1935 Moscow tournament, when the former World Champion was 67, but the competition had become much tougher after the Second World War. How was such an unexpected result possible? Smyslov never made a secret of his main chess credo. Several editions of his best games collection were entitled 'In search of harmony'. His **deep feeling for the inner harmony of the position**, which we will identify as **Trademark 1**, allowed him to play freely and easily, no matter how complicated or even bad his position was and irrespective of his age.

I met Smyslov eight times over the board when he was in his seventies. Many of those games took place during the Veterans versus Women matches that were organised by the chess Maecenas Joop van Oosterom. After two draws in 1992, I experienced the effects of his sense for harmony in the following game.

Vasily Smyslov
Judit Polgar
Monte Carlo Veterans-Women
1994 (2)

position after 25...♗d6

At this point, my advantage is beyond doubt. I have a threatening kingside majority and a perfect blocking knight on d5. On top of this, White's bishops are very passive.

Many players might be depressed by the latter condition, but to Smyslov it offered a hint about what he had to do.

26.♗c1!! During the game, I was convinced that he had played this out of despair. It later turned out that this move initiated the process of reinstating White's harmony.

Smyslov did not shy away from playing an optically 'embarrassing' move, admitting that something had gone completely wrong before.
26...h6 27.♗d2 ♖b5 28.b4 axb4 29.axb4 ♕b8

30.♗f1!! The second surprise! I do not remember a similar case when a double bishop retreat to their starting squares saved an apparently compromised position.

Suddenly, White's position is entirely playable, as his pieces work together harmoniously again. Smyslov later met my attack starting with ...g7-g5 with the queenside break b4-b5, yielding him sufficient counterplay. This change in the course of events shocked me so badly that I eventually blundered in a complicated position. (1-0, 48)

Trademark 2 – endgame specialist and... author. Studying the endgame from an early age is essential for achieving good results. When I was eight, I started studying the book on rook endings written by Levenfish and Smyslov. This more or less coincided with the time that Smyslov made his sensational comeback. Smyslov was renowned for his endgame technique and passed on much of his knowledge

In modern chess, such a performance at an advanced age is unparalleled

Winner Vasily Smyslov and his wife Nadezhda at the prize-giving of the 1956 Candidates tournament in Amsterdam. The next year he defeated Botvinnik 12½-9½.

and understanding with this book. I had learned a lot by reading it, and the next game – played a few days after the previous one – has a certain symbolic value.

Judit Polgar
Vasily Smyslov
Monte Carlo Veterans-Women
1994 (7)

position after 30.♔e2

The Berlin Defence was still several years away from becoming topical, but Smyslov had handled the opening and the game reasonably well so far, and my advantage was minimal. However, the former World Champion must have felt uncomfort-

able due to the one-sided character of the position. Hence, his next active moves.

30...♖d5 31.♖e8 ♖a5?!
This pseudo-active move is at best a waste of time. Black should have undermined my pawn majority with 31...g5.
32.a4

32...b5?
The decisive mistake. For some reason, Smyslov did not display his usual sense of harmony in this endgame.

It's true that trying to re-establish piece coordination with 32...♖d5 would be premature. My pawn majority would become threatening after 33.g4, and yield me serious winning chances.

It was not too late for 32...g5, though.

33.♖e5! Smyslov must have overlooked this move because just a couple of moves earlier, the rook had abandoned this square. Now it returns to the centre, creating a deadly pin and the threat of c3-c4.

33...♖a6 34.axb5 ♖a3 35.♖c5

My extra pawn, active rook and better structure yielded me a decisive advantage, and Smyslov resigned 20 moves later. (1-0, 55)

It gave me a funny feeling to defeat Smyslov in a rook ending. To paraphrase a saying about teachers and pupils, and also by way of a joke: had the book's reader surpassed its writer?

Trademark 3 – a **charming** presence and a **refined sense of humour**. This may be the first time in this series of articles that a 'trademark' refers to a player's personality. I make this exception not only as a gesture of veneration, but also because one of Smyslov's jokes encouraged and inspired me deeply. My aggressive and combi-

native style made him call me 'Tal in a skirt', and this gave me the motivation to follow my favourite path. In the third and last decisive game from our 'match over the years', I unleashed one of my 'trademark' attacks.

Vasily Smyslov
Judit Polgar
Prague Women-Veterans 1995 (1)

position after 23.♘e3

Strategically, White seems to be better, due to his superior structure and control of the light squares. However, the dynamic elements in the position are at least as important.

23...♕b1+ 24.♘f1?

This apparently solid move is the decisive mistake. White should have kept control of d5 with 24.♔h2, yielding him chances to defend, since the hasty 24...e4? would lose to 25.♗e8. The point is that, unlike in the game, I would not have ...♗d5.

24...e4!

25.♘3d2 ♕e1

The threat of ...♗h4 is decisive.

26.♗e8 ♗d5

27.♕a4

27.c4 would fail to gain a tempo for the defence, since it would weaken the d4-square: 27...♗d4 28.♕g3 (there is no time to take the bishop: 28.cxd5 ♕xf2+ 29.♔h2 ♕g1+ 30.♔g3 ♗e5+, with mate in sight) 28...♘f5. Unlike in the game, the knight also joins the attack. 29.♕f4 (29.♕c7+ ♔f8 /h8 wouldn't change anything) 29...e3, with decisive threats.

27...♗h4 28.g3 e3

A thematic break, clearing the long diagonal for my other bishop.

29.fxe3

In the event of 29.♕xh4 exd2, the pawn will queen.

29...♗g5

The poorly defended white king cannot resist the combined attack of my queen and bishops, so Smyslov resigned.

Conclusions

■ Develop your sense of harmony, so that you will be able to find the proper regrouping in good and bad positions alike.

■ Admitting the seriousness of the defects of one's own position may be the first step to turning things around.

■ Do not waste the chance of gaining inspiration and motivation from an inspired joke from a famous player, or simply from his charming personality. ■

MAXIMize your Tactics **Solutions**

1. Mammadov-Postny
Levitov Christmas 2020

Remember the final tiebreak game of the Carlsen-Kajakin 2016 WCh Match? **22.♕xh6+!** Black resigned as 22...♔xh6 23.♖h8 is checkmate.

2. Tabatabaei-Real de Azua
Titled Tuesday 2020

23.♘f6+! exploits the weakness of the back rank. Black resigned in view of 23...♕xf6 24.♖xf6 ♖xf6 25.♖xd8+ ♘xd8 26.♖e8 mate.

3. Gasanov-Tabatabaei
Titled Tuesday 2020

The fastest and most artistic way to conclude the attack is **20.♕xh7+! ♘xh7 21.♘xf7+** and Black resigned in view of 21...♔g8 22.♘h6 mate.

4. Fridman-Vokhidov
PNWCC Opening BI Sicilian 2020

Everything is protected in Black's camp for now, but White finds a forced sequence that opens a gateway to the enemy king: **29.♘h6+ ♔h8 30.♘g6+! hxg6 31.♘f7+ ♔g8 32.♕h8** Mate.

5. Aryan-Erigaisi
India Super Juniors 2020

25.♗g7+! draws Black's king out of the corner: **25...♖xg7 26.♖xg7 ♔xg7 27.♖g1+ ♔f8** 27...♔h8 loses to 28.♘g6+ ♔g7 29.♘e5+. **28.♕h6+ ♔e7 29.♖g7+** and White soon won.

6. Blübaum-Baskin
Titled Tuesday 2020

17.♖xe5 Less precise is 17.♘c4 dxc4 18.♗xe5 when Black at least maintains the material balance with 18...♕b4. **17...♖xe5 18.♘c4!** Black resigned as he loses the queen after 18...dxc4 19.♗xh7+.

7. Melkumyan-Duarte
RBI Open 2020

45.h6+! ♔xh6 45...♔f8 46.♘h7+; 45...♔g8 46.h7+ ♔g7 (46...♔f8 47.♕a3+ ♔g7 48.h8♕+ ♔xh8 49.♕f8 mate) 47.h8♕+ ♔xh8 48.♕xe5 loses a piece. **46.♕xe5! ♕xg5** Avoiding 46...♖xe5 47.♘xf7+ but now **47.♕h8** is mate.

8. Shahinyan-Postny
PNWCC Opening BI Sicilian 2020

15.♘xf6+! 15.♗xf6!? gxf6 16.♘e4 ♖xe4 17.♖xe4 was less forcing. **15...gxf6 16.♗d5+ ♔h8 17.♖xe8+ ♗xe8 18.♕xe8+! ♖xe8** On 18...♗f8, many moves win, the simplest is 19.♗xf6+ ♕xf6 20.♕xa8. **19.♗xf6** Mate.

9. Makhnev-Ismagambetov
Almaty 2020

41...♘g5! 42.fxg5 Now Black's queen and bishop go berserk: **42...♕e4+ 43.♖f3** 43.♔g3 ♕e3+ 44.♔h4 (44.♔g2 ♕e2+) 44...♕f2+! and mate! **43...♕e2+ 44.♔g3 ♗g1!** White resigned in view of the deadly check on h2.

How to study chess on your own

Make sure that the way you train will pay dividends

Many players lack discipline and would rather cut corners than work seriously to improve their game. **DAVORIN KULJASEVIC** believes that going the extra mile is very much worth the time and energy, as he makes a case for a structured and effective way to study chess.

How do you study chess? For example, what does your typical tactical training look like? I would guess that in most cases it involves solving a lot of tactical puzzles like this one:

Boris Spassky – Viktor Kortchnoi
Belgrade match 1978 (18)
position after 41.♕c3

Black to move and win. Can you find the solution?
I suppose it was not too difficult to find the winning move **41...♗d2!** opening files and diagonals for the final attack on the white king with tempo. This was also the move that Kortchnoi had sealed and that made Spassky immediately resign the game (and the Candidates Final match!) when he appeared for the resumption. Here is a sample line that shows how decisive the black attack is: 42.♕a3 ♗e4 43.♖h1 ♕f4 44.♖h3 ♗b4 45.♕b3 ♕g4 46.♖g3 ♗e1+!.

Undoubtedly, we all solve tactical puzzles in order to improve our skills to spot winning moves and combinations, but this is only a part of one's tactical ability. As Rudolf Spielmann famously put it: 'I can see combinations as well as Alekhine, but I cannot get to the same positions.'

Let us consider another position from the same game that preceded the one from the previous puzzle.

Boris Spassky – Viktor Kortchnoi
Belgrade 1978 (18)
position after 27.♔f2

Obviously, we have a much more complex situation here. First, some background. Spassky, playing White, was in a must-win situation, because a draw would secure match victory for Kortchnoi. Small wonder, then, that Spassky chose the sharp 27.♔f2 out of several positional alternatives to prepare the g2-g4 break.
This is a good moment to recall Spielmann's words. How did Kortchnoi manage to change the passive position in the above diagram into a winning one in little over 10 moves? Well, it takes skill to do that! Anticipating the ex-World Champion's aggressive intentions and sensing the dynamic potential of his own position, Kortchnoi devised a clever tactical ploy. He began with:

27...♕b6!?

This may be an innocent-looking move, but the idea behind it is definitely not, as we will see shortly.

28.g4 g5! It seems as if Black also has a say on the kingside. 28...fxg4?! 29.♕xg4, on the other hand, would have led to a strong attack for White.

29.hxg6 ♗xg6 30.g5

Spassky was getting ready to attack on the h-file with ♘h4, ♖h1, etc. So, here is another puzzle for you: Black to move. What would you play?

30...f4! That's it! Now it all comes together – the queen was placed on b6 to 'x-ray' the exposed white king along the g1-a7 diagonal, the rook does the same along the f-file, and the once passive light-squared bishop cuts through the b1-h7 diagonal, helping the idle knight get into the game as well.

31.exf4 ♘c2 32.♖d1

While the position remains complicated, Black clearly has the initiative. Only a couple of moves earlier, most of the black pieces were sitting on the eight rank, jobless, but now they are displaying their full dynamic potential.

In fact, Kortchnoi could have deployed his final piece with **32...♗a3!** (he went 32...♗e4), preparing to attack pawn d4 with ...♗b2.

There is no doubt in my mind that Kortchnoi had planned the sequence that started with 27...♕b6 and culminated in 30...f4! as soon as Spassky put his king on f2. It takes profound skill to conjure up such a deep tactical idea from a completely non-tactical

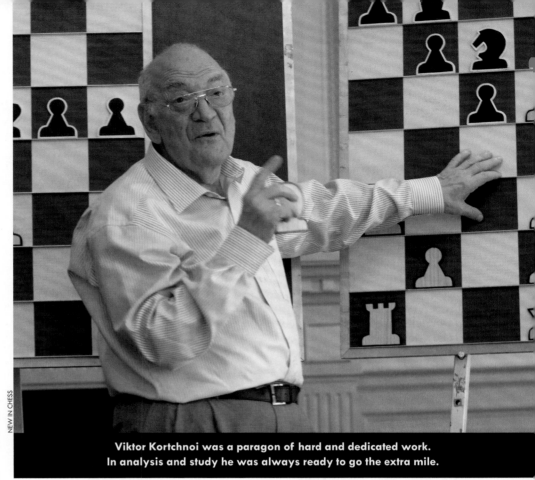

Viktor Kortchnoi was a paragon of hard and dedicated work. In analysis and study he was always ready to go the extra mile.

position. We may call it tactical vision, intuition, or a feeling for dynamics. Whatever name we attach to it, though, this ability to actively anticipate and create tactical opportunities can hardly be developed by merely solving 'Black to move and win' kind of tactical puzzles. These primarily help you to recognize opportunities and to react to tactical triggers. For such deeper understanding, a different, smarter study approach is needed.

Learning how to fish

Surprisingly, though, many chess books, even ones that claim to be 'coach yourself' guides or training

methods, are little more than puzzle or game collections, with study advice sprinkled here and there for good measure. And we are not talking only about tactics here, but about a whole range of important chess topics. Such books only scratch the surface by providing the study material, but they rarely provide a systematic explanation of the most effective approaches and methods to study that material. To paraphrase the well-known Chinese proverb, the authors of such books give chess players fish instead of teaching them how to fish. Yet, in order to maximize one's learning effects, it is essential for anyone who is ambitious about

To paraphrase the well-known Chinese proverb, the authors of such books give chess players fish instead of teaching them how to fish

their chess to develop solid and independent study habits. In other words, to continue the analogy, to learn how to fish on their own.

Develop your internal resources

Let us take a practical example. We all read chess books. When you play over examples from a book, how deeply do you study them? My educated guess is that most people mainly follow the variations that are provided by the author, rarely stopping to consider alternatives or challenge the author's assumptions. However, if you would like to get the most out of your learning experience, it is essential that you actively ask questions about what you are reading. Take, for instance, the following position from the book *Positional Decision Making in Chess* by Boris Gelfand:

Boris Gelfand – Daniel Campora
Izmir EU-Cup 2004
position after 30.♔f2

White has a clear endgame advantage, thanks to his space advantage and Black's weak pawn a6-pawn. In the game, Campora continued
30...♘c5
and then Gelfand created an endgame masterpiece after 31.♔e3 ♔e7 32.b4! ♘cd7 33.♗h3!, stopping ...f7-f5 for good and dooming Black to eternal passivity (1-0, 57).
However, in his notes to 30...♘c5, Gelfand wrote: 'Still, I cannot shake the idea that if Black had played
30...f5
I am not absolutely sure I could have won the game. I would have to show great technique, put the bishop on

c8, manoeuvre the knight around and see what happened. It's probably winning, but I do not feel the same degree of certainty.'
Since Gelfand did not provide any further variations, this is a perfect moment to put the book aside and analyse the position yourself to find out whether it is indeed winning or not.
31.♗h3 fxe4 32.fxe4 ♔e7 33.♔f3 ♘f6

The key difference with the game is that the f6-square is available to the knight. Not only does this provide Black with extra manoeuvring space, but it also deprives the white king of the g4-square, which was instrumental in the breakthrough in the game. I looked at several plans for White here, including those that Gelfand mentioned in his game notes (♗c8; manoeuvre the knight; sacrifice on a6 or b5), but Black seems to be as solid as a rock with a relatively straightforward defence. My later analysis with an engine only confirmed that conclusion.
34.♘d3
34.♗f5 ♘bd7 35.g4 may even be met by 35...g5, since Black is in time to cover the f5-square: 36.b4 ♘e8 37.♘e2 ♘g7 38.♘g3 ♘b8 39.♗c8 ♔d8 40.♗f5 ♔e7, with equality. On the other hand, the attempt to sacrifice a piece wouldn't work: 34.b4 ♘bd7 35.♘e2 ♔d8 36.♘c3 ♘f8 37.♗f1 g5 38.♘xb5?? axb5 39.♗xb5 ♔c7, and Black wins.
34...♘fd7!
The other knight needs to remain on b8 to keep the a-pawn covered.

35.b4 While this move stops ...♘c5, it also takes away the b4-outpost from the knight, limiting White's options. White would love to play 35.♔g4?! but it is not a good idea here in view of 35...♘c5 36.♘xc5 dxc5.
35...♗f6 36.♗f5 ♘bd7

Now, if White tries to send the knight towards the f5-square with **37.♘e1 ♔d8 38.♘g2** then Black can set up an impenetrable defensive set-up with **38...♘f8 39.h4 g6 40.♗h3 h5 41.g4 hxg4+ 42.♗xg4 ♘xg4 43.♔xg4 ♘h7**

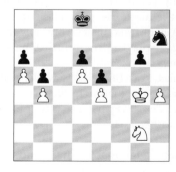

And it's a draw.

So, objectively speaking, the endgame after 30...f5 seems to be drawn. However, a more important takeaway

When you study chess on your own, you should try to have as many such independent thinking moments as possible

from this example is that you should always keep a healthy dose of curiosity while studying chess and feel free to clarify your doubts through independent analysis. Whatever conclusion you arrive at, the analytical process itself will 'improve your understanding of the game and sharpen your intuition,' as Gelfand noted somewhere else in his exceptional book.

When you study chess on your own, you should try to have as many such independent thinking moments as possible. These are the ones that make the difference, as they help you develop your internal resources. It is important to realize that external study resources (good quality chess books, videos, software, magazines, and even chess lessons with strong coaches – no matter how good and numerous they are) will hardly help you achieve your chess potential if you don't put a genuine effort into developing your internal resources.

Real quality should come from within; from the way you analyse positions and think about various problems in chess, from the curiosity with which you ask questions and the creativity of your solutions. Unlike the external ones, your internal resources are free and always available to you. And most importantly, they are just about your only ally when you sit down to play a game of chess.

Therefore, it is well worth developing study habits that foster them, such as:
■ Spending several training sessions studying typical middlegame structures that arise from an important opening tabiya. For example, this one

from the Breyer Variation of the Ruy Lopez:

position after 16...c4

■ Taking an hour or two to independently analyse an interesting middlegame fragment, for example:

Vladimir Tukmakov – Zdenko Kozul
Solin/Split 2000
position after 20...dxe5

■ Consulting the 'Similar Endgames' tool in ChessBase to research endgames that catch your attention, e.g.:

Levon Aronian – Vishy Anand
Zurich 2014
position after 58.♖xb5

I am fully aware that these and other, similar study methods will never be

as sexy as 'puzzle-rushing', 'wood-pecking', and more of such crowd-pleasers. However, when done diligently over a period of time, such thoughtful practices will improve your chess understanding and, consequently, your strength the most.

This kind of chess study requires you to have a long-term outlook, process the chess material that comes your way fairly deeply, and be ready to get out of your comfort zone often. It is not a walk in the park, but, as any strong chess player will tell you, it is worth it.

Mr. Bean's solution

Sometimes, chess players may not even be aware of how they are cutting corners while studying chess. They will memorize variations from an opening course, convinced that they 'understand' the opening well, without going to the trouble of studying strategic subtleties of the ensuing middlegames on their own.

They will do a quick post-game analysis with an engine, obtaining 'full clarity' about the game, instead of doing a more thorough analysis at home.

The list goes on and the common theme is 'getting the job done' instead of engaging your internal resources deeply into the study process. This outcome-oriented study mindset reminds me of an amusing episode of the Mr. Bean TV series in which the main character, after unsuccessfully trying to fall asleep, decides to count sheep on a painting on the wall. However, instead of getting sleepy while counting, he gets annoyed as he repeatedly loses count of the sheep and has to start all over again. Suddenly, he gets the great idea to skip the tedious counting process altogether, instead taking out a... calculator(!) and multiplying the number of sheep in the first row with those in the first column. As the total sheep count finally appears on the calculator screen, Mr. Bean, obviously relieved, murmurs: 'Oh!' and immediately drops back on his pillow and falls asleep! Job done!

Use the computer in your head

Our silicon assistants are apparently not only good at helping us fall asleep, but also at lulling our mind into a false sense of comprehension. No one knows this better than chess players, because they spend countless hours analysing with chess engines. Of course, engines are fantastic study tools that have helped us enormously to improve our overall understanding of the game. However, if you reach the point where you are more comfortable consulting zeroes and decimal points on the screen than using your own reasoning and judgement, you may have a problem. Over-reliance on engines is a modern illness with an old-school remedy: always look at a position with your own eyes before turning on the almighty machine. Not only is this crucial for the development of your inner resources, it is also stimulating to see how human logic and intuition can sometimes produce strong ideas that an engine cannot, as in the following example:

Robert Zelcic – Marin Bosiocic
Zagreb 2019
(position from analysis)

White's last try in the analysis was 24.f4 (in the game, 24.b3 was played), trying to exploit the position of the black rook. The threat is 25.g4, with either 26.fxe5 or 26.f5 as a follow-up, depending on how Black continues. What would you play here as Black? When you think about this position, some obvious ideas pop up, e.g. 24... h5, to simply prevent White's threat, or 24...♔f7 25.g4 ♔e6!? to centralize the king. Black has several other

reasonable moves, but it is interesting to note that Stockfish's third candidate is 24...b6 – a move that makes very little sense from a human point of view.

Looking at this position with my own eyes, though, I came up with an interesting idea.

24...g5!?

This move is not even among Stockfish's five top choices on depth 30, yet it is quite interesting and even – ambitious! The point is to meet

25.g4

with an exchange sacrifice:

25...♖xf4 26.♗xf4 gxf4

For the exchange, Black gets three connected passed pawns in the centre. White can block them for the moment, but if the blockade is somehow lifted, the pawns could become very dangerous. Of course, this was an intuitive sacrifice based on my initial assessment that Black would have enough compensation. I happened to analyse this position together with a young student with a rating of around 2000 FIDE, so we made a couple of natural moves for both sides to try to understand the position better.

27.♔g2

When I checked this position with the engine after our analysis, it suggested a better, more active plan for White: 27.♖d3! ♔f7 28.♖h3, although even here, after, for example, 28...b6! 29.♖b1 d5 30.♖h5 e4! 31.♖f5+ ♖f6 32.♖xd5 f3 we can see the full potential of Black's connected passed pawns.

27...♔f7 28.♖ad1 ♔e6 29.♔f3

Both sides have centralized their pieces, but I was starting to get a feeling that White might be having a difficult time finding a constructive plan, whereas Black has active ideas like ...b7-b5-b4 and ...♖c4. So I asked my student how he would evaluate this position – who is better? I am not sure who was more surprised – him, when he heard the question, or me, when I received a resolute: 'White' (with a hint of 'Are you seriously asking this question?' in his voice) by way of an answer. However, as we continued to analyse this endgame for a few more moves, it transpired that White's case was far harder to defend than he had thought.

29...b5 30.♖5d3 ♖c4 31.♔e2

Another line of our analysis went: 31.b3 e4+ 32.♔xf4 ♗g5+! 33.♔g3 exd3 34.bxc4 bxc4 and, interestingly, Black wins thanks to the connected passers on the queenside!

31...a5 32.a3 b4 33.axb4 axb4

The initiative is already firmly in Black's hands and White has to tread carefully to even save the game!

After our analysis, I was pretty convinced of the soundness of the exchange sacrifice. However, when I checked it with the engine afterwards, its initial evaluation after 24... g5 was close to 1.00 for White! Naturally, I wanted to understand why the engine was so pessimistic about Black's chances, so I fed it a few more moves. And then, an interesting thing happened – the machine gradually decreased its positive evaluation of White's position until it was at 0.00 on the move 29.♔f3. Further analysis proved that my intuitive assessment

HOW TO STUDY CHESS ON YOUR OWN

was right – Black has full compensation for the exchange, even with some upside potential with the connected passed pawns if White makes even a slight mistake.

The main thing to take away from this example is that you want to make sure that you use your own mind in the analysis first – an interesting idea like 24...g5!? 25.g4 ♖xf4 would not have occurred to you if you had turned on the engine first.

Study with structure

We all know that guy, the soul of every chess club. Let's call him Mark. In group analysis, Mark is usually the first one to suggest a move and is quick to explain why his brilliant idea works. He loves to attack, and he loves studying gambits and sharp opening variations. Mark also happily skips the analysis of a positional game or a theoretical endgame to play some blitz. A lot of it, to be more precise.

One thing, however, that you may have noticed about Mark, if you have known him long enough, is that his chess has not improved all that much over the years. He did have a great

tournament last winter, beating a couple of titled players, but then he lost 100 rating points in his next two tourneys. While undoubtedly a talented chess player, Mark seems to be quite inconsistent. You have studied chess at his home a couple of times, typically agreeing beforehand to analyse games from a book on Petrosian together or to play a thematic Nimzo-Indian sparring match; but somehow you would always end up looking at his favourite Traxler Gambit, watching chess streams on Twitch while sipping on beer, or playing bullet, instead.

You have come to realize that Mark's inconsistent results might largely be a result of a lack of structure in his studies. He is not good at organizing his chess study time, nor at picking the right study topics or resources. Most importantly, he simply cannot make himself study things that he does not like studying.

It is safe to say that most of us can be like Mark from time to time, and that's okay. Chess study should have elements of spontaneity and fun, otherwise why do it? However, some-

times it requires hard work to, say, iron out your opening repertoire, improve your manoeuvring skills in closed positions, or upgrade your endgame technique. In such cases, you might want to commit to a plan that will help you organize your study activities and time better – a purposeful structure. Setting goals, planning weekly study schedules, and completing daily to-do lists can go a long way towards making you more focused and productive.

Now, I am sure that you also know a player like Tom. Tom plays chess for the same club as Mark. He has never been considered a particularly talented chess player, but he has been improving quite steadily lately. He always had a knack for positional play, while tactics was not his strong suit. In fact, Mark would often swindle Tom in friendly games from rather suspicious positions. After realizing that he needed to work on this area of his game to get better, Tom devised a two-month study plan focusing on improving his tactical play. Here is what his typical three-hour study day looked like:
1. Solve tactical puzzles from online tactics trainers or a tactics book for 30 minutes.
2. Solve a couple of endgame studies and/or chess problems in blindfold mode for another 30 minutes.
3. Analyse a sharp game from an advanced tactics book for one hour.
4. Do a 'find the best move' simulation of a game of a tactical role-model player for one hour.

Mark also happily skips the analysis of a positional game or a theoretical endgame to play some blitz. A lot of it, to be more precise

He feels that the game is heating up and every time he goes for a walk, Tom hits him with some unexpected move

Once or twice a week, Tom would also ask a friend to play out a couple of online sparring games from a predetermined double-edged position. He particularly enjoyed the post-mortem analysis of these games. Tom also made a promise to himself to do tactical training every single day during this two-month period, even while commuting by train, when he was tired, or not in the mood. This way, he wanted to make sure that he would be in 'tactics mode' for his next big tournament. And, as fate would have it, in the third round of the tournament, he met his club colleague Mark, always an unpleasant opponent.

Mark
Tom
Welcome back to OTB tournament, 2021 (3)
Ruy Lopez, Keres Defence

1.e4 e5 2.♘f3 ♘c6 3.♗b5 a6 4.♗a4 ♘f6 5.0-0 ♗e7 6.♖e1 b5 7.♗b3 d6 8.c3 0-0 9.h3 ♘a5 10.♗c2 c5 11.d4 ♘d7 12.♔h1 ♖b8 13.d5 ♘b6

The game began peacefully enough, after which, as expected, Mark did not waste time making his attacking ambitions known, charging forward with his favourite Ruy Lopez move:

14.g4

'All right, I am going for ♖g1, ♘bd2-f1-g3, and if he plays ...g6, I will prepare the ♘f5-sacrifice. Tom will probably try something on the queenside, but whatever it is, I am going to mate him. Time to go for a walk!' Mark thought to himself as

he confidently got up from his chair. Meanwhile, Tom had indeed briefly considered preparing queenside counterplay with ...♗d7, ...♘b7, ...c4 and ...♘c5, but then he remembered analysing a game between Fischer and Keres a while ago, in which Keres played ...h5 in response to Fischer's g4 in a similar position. 'This could be risky if he takes on h5 and plays ♖g1, but let's check it,' reasoned Tom. Five minutes passed, then 10, then 20, and Tom still hadn't made his move. Mark, who had already checked all the other games in progress, grew increasingly pleased. 'He doesn't know what to do against my attack,' he whispered to a mutual friend who stopped by their table. Suddenly, a piece moved – and not the one that Mark had expected...

14...h5!? 'What kind of a move is that? Is he trying to get killed?' thought Mark, as he glanced over to the unusually calm Tom and hesitantly wrote the move on the scoresheet. After a couple of minutes, still unsure what his opponent was up to, he played:

15.gxh5 'He takes on h3, I play ♖g1, he should move his king to h8, and then I'll go ♘g5. A great position! I knew that this was the right way to play against Tom. He just can't handle attacks.' But then, much to his surprise, Tom quickly replied:

15...♕d7!

'Hmm... so he probably prepared this move. Okay, h3 is hanging, but I can still go ♖g1 – I will simply cover my king with ♘h2. It doesn't seem like he has anything better than ...♔h8 after

that, anyway, so I can keep attacking. Let's go for it!'

16.♖g1 ♕xh3+ 17.♘h2

Once again, Mark stood up from his chair with an obvious air of satisfaction. His attack should unfold naturally now, ♖g3 providing a tempo on the queen, followed by ♕g1 or ♔g2, ♘f3... Only, Tom had different plans. After another 10 minutes of reflection, he concluded that the follow-up that he had considered before going 14...h5 was definitely viable. So he proceeded with:

17...f5!

In fact, this move had also occurred to Mark, as he was walking around the playing hall, but he was sure that Tom, 'a safe player', would never play this. Now, back at the table, he was getting perplexed by the way that the game had unfolded. 'I guess that he is just going all-out against me. But this cannot be right, g7 is so weak. I can definitely play 18.h6... Wait, can I sacrifice on g7?' Mark calculates 18.♖xg7+ for a couple of minutes, but ends up with the somewhat disappointing conclusion that it is only good for a draw. 'Okay, so it seems I should play 18.h6 after all. He has to defend with ...♖f7, but I'm definitely keeping the initiative there.' So he pushes the pawn:

18.h6?

... although this time he does not leave his chair. He feels that the game is heating up and whether he is being superstitious or not, every time he goes for a walk, Tom hits him with some unexpected move. Time to dig in and calculate some lines!

On the other side of the board, Tom is seriously considering sacrificing a piece with 18...f4. It is not entirely clear to him how strong this sacrifice is, but it feels promising. It reminds him of some attacking positions from Smirin's *King's Indian Warfare* that he had analysed recently. Realizing that this might be the critical moment of the game, Tom takes 15 minutes to carefully calculate critical variations. And so, eventually he plays:

18...f4! Mark is in a state of shock. 'A free piece – no way! Tom is surely up to something.' However, there is not much choice at this point but to accept the sacrifice, it seems. If he takes on g7 with the pawn, Black will already start attacking with ...♖f6-h6. 'Well, let's take the piece and see where it leads. I am a bit undeveloped, and my rook will be awkward on e7, but if the worst came to the worst and things became tricky, I could give back some material. It's not as if he has a forced mate or something.'

19.♖xg7+ ♚h8 20.♖xe7 ♕xh6

While deliberating about whether to push 18...f4, Tom was pleased to find that he would have the threat of a strong double attack with 21...♖g8, followed by 22...♕g5, since the rook on e7 is loose. Mark was arriving at that same conclusion, only a

couple of moves too late. Black's attack seemed very strong in virtually all variations that he had calculated after the most natural move 21.♘d2, and he just couldn't find a way to untangle his pieces. But then, suddenly, a tactical idea hit Mark like a bolt of lightning: 'Good or bad, I have to open the position. The Spanish bishop has to live!' And so, without giving it a second thought, he rushed to play:

21.♗d3 ♖g8 22.♗xf4?!

Mark felt proud for finding this idea in a difficult position. If the queen took on f4, he would give checkmate with 23.♕h5+.

And after **22...exf4,** which was Tom's move, he blitzed out **23.e5**

The ♖h7+ threat had seemed very promising to Mark from afar. Initially he thought that Black would have to prevent it with 23...♖g7, when he would have a couple of pleasant choices. However, as the position appeared on the board, he realized that things might not be so rosy after all. The move 23...♖b7, which he had failed to consider, seemed to parry his threat in a much more convenient way for Black. Mark realized that Black was better in that position, yet he still harboured some hope of saving the game, when Tom hit him, once again, with an unexpected move:

23...♗h3! ... and – for the first time in the game – left his seat. He had calculated the winning variation right up to the end. 'That's a strong move,' muttered Mark to himself.

'I had totally missed that one.' Still unsure as to how the game had got out of hand so quickly, he delivered his first and last check of the game:
24.♖h7+ ♕xh7 25.♗xh7 ♗g2+ 26.♚g1 ♗f3+ 27.♗xg8 ♖xg8+ 28.♚f1 ♗xd1 29.exd6 f3

It was time to resign.

After the game, as they walked out of the playing hall together, Mark remarked: 'Honestly, Tom, I had not expected that you would crush me like that. Where did that come from?'

'Well, I worked a bit on my tactics recently', Tom replied modestly. 'You did, huh?' said Mark with a surprised expression on his face. 'Did you solve a lot of puzzles or what?' and then, without waiting for a reply, he inserted: 'By the way, I really like Puzzle Storm on lichess. What's your record there?'

'I guess I did some extra work on the puzzles...' Tom answered, ignoring the second question, '... although, you know what, you might want to read an article in *New In Chess*...' Mark raised his eyebrows as Tom continued: 'It is about chess study. I could lend you my copy.' ∎

In his new book **How to Study Chess on Your Own: Creating a Plan that Works... and Sticking to it!** *(New In Chess), Davorin Kuljasevic provides a solid self-study framework that offers anyone, from casual player to chess professional, a multitude of original learning methods and valuable practical ideas for improving yourself.*

Of the Modernized Modern and the Elephant Gambit

As we keep our fingers crossed that one day soon the lockdowns may be lifted and we can sit down at the board again, brushing up on our openings sounds like a good plan. **MATTHEW SADLER** has already set to work and discovered that the repertoires on offer are often quite, eh, ... different!

After a year of weariness for opening theory, I've suddenly started devouring opening books again. Maybe the growing feeling that the end of the lockdown is in sight and that over-the-board chess might return in some shape or form this year has panicked my chess brain into wanting to know again how the game starts. And for a man with a craving for opening theory, there is no shortage of material for addiction! Our selection this time is towards the offbeat and unpopular, but each of these openings gets the full analytical treatment that in the old days used to be reserved for the 6.♗g5 Najdorf! For instance, 416 beautifully-produced pages of dense analysis on the Elephant Gambit (1.e4 e5 2.♘f3 d5) from a major publishing house is kind of par for the course nowadays!

We start off with another book in Thinkers Publishing's 'Modern-ized' series, from the English Grand-master Daniel Fernandez, this time examining... the Modern! I reviewed Daniel's previous book for Thinkers Publishing on the Caro-Kann favour-ably and *The Modernized Modern Defence* shares the same character-istics: plenty of risky lines, a lot of original thinking and some unusual recommendations.

Let me start off by saying that for those qualities alone, this is a book I would recommend to anyone who either plays or faces the Modern: you'll find plenty of ideas for your own games. However, I was at times a little confused by the presentation of the material: in essence I think a short chapter on move transpositions would have done the book a world of good.

The key point in a Modern reper-toire is where (or whether) you make the crossover to other openings, sometimes to the King's Indian (when White plays 1.e4 g6 2.d4 ♗g7 3.c4) and most crucially to the Pirc (when Black decides he can delay ...♘f6 no longer). In the first chapter of Part II, Fernandez identifies a subtle White move order delaying ♘c3 via 1.e4 g6 2.d4 ♗g7 3.♘f3 d6 and now either 4.♗e2 or 4.♗e3. This flexible move order dissuades Black from trying the typical Modern plan of 4...a6 (aiming for quick queenside devel-opment with ...b5, ...♗b7. ...♘d7 and ...c5) due to 5.c4, when Black will end up in a King's Indian where the odd ...a6 has been played rather early. For that reason, Black will likely respond 4...♘f6, when 5.♘c3 prods Black into the Pirc and away from the Modern.

This is an important observation, but it is not made very clearly. I felt I only grasped what Fernandez meant because I knew it already (3.♗e3 d6 4.♕d2 is another way of doing this, which I remember discussing with Nigel Short some years ago. White even keeps the option of heading back into a Sämisch with f3 and then c4). As it is, the aspiring Modern player may spend some time wondering why ♗e3 systems are dealt with in Part II Chapter 1 and Part IV Chapter 3 (not to mention Part III Chapter 3).

The other doubt I had was the dodginess of some of the lines! Maybe if I had read *The Exhilarating*

Maybe the growing feeling that over-the-board chess might return this year has panicked my chess brain into wanting to know again how the game starts

Elephant Gambit first, then I would have been desensitized to dodginess! It's also perhaps a moot point whether it's appropriate to complain about risk in a book about the Modern. However, a few lines tickled my spidey-sense while reading through without a board such as this one:
1.e4 g6 2.d4 ♗g7 3.♘c3 d6 4.♗e3 a6 5.a4 ♘f6 6.f3 c6 7.♕d2 0-0 8.h4 h5 9.g4 hxg4 10.0-0-0 gxf3 11.♘xf3 b5

Fernandez notes that 'as this is one of the few lines in the book where I advocate castling into it and running a considerable risk of getting mated immediately, I've been quite careful with examining all the forcing alternatives'. From the Black side, I was already curled up in a ball and crying to be honest, but I decided to use this line as calculation practice. Firstly, 12.h5 is extremely scary, but, more importantly, White can throw in 11.h5,

which I'd noted as a candidate move as well as 11.♘xf3.
It looked very fraught to me but I was still shocked to see +3.62 as the evaluation when I checked my analysis with my engines! Daniel suggests

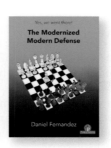

The Modernized Modern Defence
Daniel Fernandez
Thinkers Publishing, 2020
★★★☆☆

The Richter-Rauzer Reborn
The Kozul Variation
Zdenko Kozul and Alozije Jankovic
Thinkers Publishing, 2019
★★★☆☆

other possible approaches, so you're not stuck with this line, but there are a few lines like this that you need to check carefully. To be honest, even if this line had held together somehow, I would never have wanted to risk it in a practical game.
In summary therefore, full of interest but of most immediate use as extra inspiration for someone who knows the Modern well already! 3 stars!

■ ■ ■

The Richter-Rauzer Reborn. The Kozul Variation by Zdenko Kozul and Alozije Jankovic (Thinkers Publishing) takes a detailed look at the sub-variation of the Richter-Rauzer that bears Kozul's name:
1.e4 c5 2.♘f3 d6 3.d4 cxd4 4.♘xd4 ♘f6 5.♘c3 ♘c6 6.♗g5 e6 7.♕d2 a6 8.0-0-0 ♗d7.

Why should this variation bear his name I hear you ask? Well... dating back to 1984, Kozul has played an astonishing 212 games as Black in this line (in my database alone), with a score of just over 50% and a rating performance of 2525... So, he absolutely deserves it!
The author obviously has a vast amount of practical knowledge to draw upon and states in the introduc-

tion that 'I will mention again that, as before, with the necessity of using the help of the engine, the emphasis was always on the practical aspect of the position. Very often, therefore, our assessment of the position as well as suggestions for further play were not just the result of the engine's advice, but our practical estimation based on years of experience and tournament advice'.
The book is essentially in two parts: the first part looks at 9.f3 and the second part at 9.f4. The latter move leads to typical Richter-Rauzer positions, where White often gives up the bishop pair with ♗xf6 to give Black doubled f-pawns.
It's an interesting book which examines difficult, unusual positions and there are indeed some types of positions which engines assess as strong for White but where the authors give grounds for a more nuanced assessment (particularly positions with opposite-coloured bishops). However, my impres-

Particularly suggestions that are off the beaten track need to be examined carefully before attempting them in practice

sion is that the positions are essentially quite fraught, and particularly suggestions that are off the beaten track need to be examined carefully before attempting them in practice. For example, my attention was drawn to an idea (14...♖a7) Kozul calls 'a bit strange' from the game **Carlsen-Kotronias, Mallorca 2004**, in the chapter on the main line with 13.f5:

1.e4 c5 2.♘f3 d6 3.d4 cxd4 4.♘xd4 ♘f6 5.♘c3 ♘c6 6.♗g5 e6 7.♕d2 a6 8.0-0-0 ♗d7 9.f4 b5 10.♗xf6 gxf6 11.♔b1 ♕b6 12.♘xc6 ♗xc6 13.f5 ♕c5 14.♗d3 ♖a7

It felt a bit dodgy to unprotect the d8-square, with the white queen and rook doubled on the d-file, so my heart leapt a little at the prospect of 15.e5, which looked pretty worrying for Black (15...♕xe5 16.♖he1!), but I was again shocked at the scale of the engine evaluations: more than +2!
15.e5 fxe5 15...dxe5 16.♘e4 ♕e7 17.♕f2 (threatening ♘xf6+ and fxe6) 17...♗xe4 18.♗xe4 ♖c7 19.♕f3 followed by ♗c6+ looks awful for Black, as the white rooks will soon double on the d-file and invade on the seventh or eighth ranks.
16.♕g5 A very unpleasant move, threatening ♕f6 followed by fxe6.
16...♗e7 17.♕h6 exf5 18.♗xf5 ♖f8 19.♗e4

This is also a nightmare for Black, as White will capture on h7, establish a minor piece on d5 and then push the h-pawn.
After 15.e5, the engine matches I ran between Stockfish 13 and Komodo Dragon ended in 10 straight wins for White!

In summary, for me just like the Fernandez book on the Modern: plenty of interesting material from an experienced practitioner of the opening, but care required in following some of the lines in the book! 3 stars!

■ ■ ■

I've mentioned it a few times already and here it is: *The Exhilarating Elephant Gambit* by Jakob Aabling-Thomsen & Michael Agermose Jensen (Quality Chess). Hundreds of pages dedicated to the joy of being a central pawn down after 3 moves! 1.e4 e5 2.♘f3 d5 3.exd5.

On the other hand, we've seen plenty of books about the Morra Gambit, so why not the Elephant!?
The book is divided into 3 parts. Part 1 deals with 3.♘xe5, Part 2 with the most challenging reply 3.exd5 and Part 3 with the odds and ends such as 3.♘c3. It's an extremely well-researched and enthusiastically-written book, whose tone reminds me somewhat of the books the legendary English IM Michael Basman (75 today as I write this, Happy Birthday Mike!) produced on the St. George (1...a6, 2...b5). After reading those books, you simply could not imagine a better

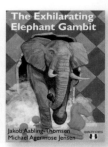

The Exhilarating Elephant Gambit Jakob Aabling-Thomsen & Michael Agermose Jensen Quality Chess, 2020
★★★★☆

system... an illusion that lasted right up to the moment you played them!

I've been pointing out dodgy lines in the previous opening books I've reviewed, but that really seems to be missing the point with an opening as this one! I'll just say that the authors do a great job of squeezing out the maximum from Black's position and manage to make a convincing case for counterplay in most of the lines. I guess that my practical reservations about the book would be on the value of the effort you have to spend. Once people know you play it, then the chances increase of getting Stockfish's main line on the board all the time, which is anything but pleasant for Black. On the other hand, mastering the 400 pages of the book just to use it as a one-time surprise weapon is a luxury that only professionals can afford.
However, a brief read of the book gave me an additional fun and high-scoring weapon in blitz (it is a particularly useful weapon against pre-moving Italian Game practi-

Hundreds of pages dedicated to the joy of being a central pawn down after 3 moves!

tioners: 1.e4 e5 2.♘f3 d5 3.♗c4!) and, since that's the only chess most of us are getting right now, this is probably as useful a book for the Internet age as any! Good fun, good weapon for blitz, 4 stars!

■ ■ ■

1.e4 vs Minor Defences is the latest instalment of Parimarjan Negi's 1.e4 series for Quality Chess. This book presents a complete repertoire against the Alekhine, the Scandinavian, the Pirc, the Modern, 1...♘c6, 1...b6 and a few other odds and ends. What impressed me enormously about previous volumes was the mix of deep engine analysis and grandmasterly reasoning that Negi applied to his opening recommendations. A substantial number of Negi's lines diverged from the engine top recommendations, but where he followed the engine, he spent a considerable amount of time explaining the logic behind the move. I was happy to see that the trend has continued in this volume!

A good example of this are Negi's suggested lines against Owen's defence (1...b6).

1.e4 b6 2.d4 ♗b7 3.♘c3 e6 4.♘f3 ♗b4 5.♗d3 ♘f6

Here Negi proposes two interesting sacrifices: 6.♕e2 d5 7.0-0 ♗xc3 8.e5

and 6.e5 ♘e4 7.0-0 ♘xc3 8.bxc3 ♗xc3 9.♗g5.

Throwing rather powerful cloud hardware against these lines through

1.e4 vs Minor Defences
Parimarjan Negi
Quality Chess, 2020
★★★★★

1500 Forced Mates
Jakov Geller
Elk and Ruby, 2021
★★★★☆

the Chessify engine service, you see that the engines' assessments of Negi's lines (Leela Zero and Stockfish) converge to between 0.03 and 0.15, which is an assessment which could lead you to dismiss

Where Negi follows the engine, he spends a considerable amount of time explaining the logic behind the move

the lines as uninteresting for study. However, Negi makes a good case for the practical difficulties involved for the Black player in the resulting positions in each line, and the engine matches I've run from these positions between Stockfish 13 and Komodo Dragon show that there is a welcome amount of imbalance in the positions.

This book is an extremely well-worked out grandmaster repertoire that balances engine and correspondence experience with a good feeling for the needs of the practical player. I try and hold myself in a bit more nowadays with 5-star ratings, but this one deserves it! 5 stars!

■ ■ ■

1500 Forced Mates by Jakov Geller (Elk and Ruby) is the surprise package of this month's reviews! This book does exactly what it says on the cover, bringing together 1500 forced mating combinations, the first 1380 – normally focusing on just one mating theme – being relatively simple (most take me a just a glance to solve them,

with a few exceptions... see later!), while the last chapter is a bit tougher, bringing together several different themes in one puzzle. All the positions are composed (not from actual games, although the positions look as if they do come from practical play) and, according to the author, the puzzles have the following characteristics: they increase gradually in difficulty, none are unsolvable and there are a minimum number of alternative solutions.

I started solving the puzzles a little aimlessly at first but found myself getting surprisingly addicted! I've gone through 796 already and I'm sure I'll be working through the rest in the next week. It's simply an extremely easy and pleasant way to sharpen your tactical skills: puzzle rush for the non-digital chess player! It's the clarity of the solutions that appeals. Once you understand the required tactical theme, the execution is reasonably obvious and always 100% decisive, which gives you maximum reward for your efforts!

As I said, most of the puzzles I've solved so far have been easy for me (mind you, Matthew Sadler's rating is 2694... – ed.), but one stinker so far had me straining my brain for an unreasonable amount of time. It reminds me enormously of the shogi tsume puzzles I've been solving in preparation for the coming season of the World Shogi League (when the GB2-Denmark top board match-up in November might also feature a certain Peter-Heine... ☺). Those are very much about blocking escape squares with sacrifices, and this one is a fine chess equivalent! I'll put the solution at the end of the article if you want to try and solve it yourselves.

White to play and mate

Great fun and very useful for your tactics! 4 stars!

■ ■ ■

And, finally, a lovely book for which I didn't need to fire up the heavy engines or even rack my brains too much but could just enjoy reading! *The Chess Saga of Fridrik Olafsson* looks back on the career of former World Championship Candidate and ex-FIDE President Fridrik Olafsson. Olafsson's career as a professional chess player was quite short. He came to prominence in the mid-1950s but retired from chess to study law in 1964, becoming the world's strongest amateur player! In that brief 10-year period, he defeated many of the world's top players and qualified from the 1958 Portoroz Interzonal to play in the famous 1959 Candidates tournament. Although his result of 7th out of 8 (he scored 10 points, well behind the winner Tal, who scored 20!) was relatively disappointing, this is still a career peak of which any chess player would be very proud! Now 86, he's still looking fit and going strong judging from the picture in the book!

The annotations to many of the games stem from Olafsson's commentaries in the 1970s with light corrections from modern engines. The book itself is a beautiful hardback, with many photos and tournament tables. Olafsson was

The Chess Saga of Fridrik Olafsson
Oystein Brekke,
Fridrik Olafsson
Norsk Sjakkforlag,
2021
★★★★☆

a player of attacking bent, which also makes the games – many of which were unknown to me – very pleasurable to play through!

I'll leave you with Olafsson's game against New Zealander Bob Wade which he considered to be the best attacking game of his career.

Bob Wade
Fridrik Olafsson
Hastings 1953/54
King's Indian Defence

1.d4 ♘f6 2.c4 g6 3.♘c3 ♗g7 4.e4 0-0 5.♗e3 d6 6.h3 e5 7.d5 ♘bd7 8.♗d3 ♘h5 9.g3 ♘c5 10.♗c2 a5 11.♕e2 ♗d7 12.0-0-0 a4 13.♘f3 ♕c8 14.♖dg1 a3 15.b3 ♘a6 16.♕d2 ♖e8 17.♘h4 ♘b4 18.♗d1 ♘f6 19.g4 c6 20.g5

20...♘fxd5 21.♘xd5 ♘xd5 22.exd5 cxd5 23.♕xd5 b5
White has won a piece, but the move 20.g5 has rendered the knight on h4 offside and useless. With the pawn on g4, White could at least dream of an attack with ♘f5!. White fights desperately to keep some grip in the centre and to disrupt Black's attacking play by exchanging off queens.
24.♗f3 e4 25.♗xe4 ♖a6

Threatening ...♗c6 winning the bishop on e4.
26.♕b7 Will White manage to swap off the queens?
26...♖xe4 No!
27.♕xe4 bxc4

28.b4 ♗b2+ 29.♔b1 d5 30.♕xd5 ♖d6 A great move! 31.♕xd6 is met by 31...♗f5+, with mate.
31.♕e4 c3 32.♖c1 ♗c6 33.♕c4 ♕b7 Threatening ...♗xh1 as well as ...♗e4+. **34.f3 ♗b5 35.♕f4 ♗d3+ 36.♖c2 ♕d5**

37.♖h2
Here 37.♕h2 was what Olafsson was hoping for, when 37...♕xa2+ 38.♔xa2 ♗c4+ 39.♔b1 a2 is mate!
37...♗c4 38.♖xb2 axb2 39.♖xb2 ♕d1+ 40.♗c1 ♗d3+ 0-1.

In summary, a beautifully produced and pleasurable book to read through! 4 stars! ■

Solution:
1.♖g6+ fxg6 (1...♔xg6 2.♕g2+ ♔f5 3.♖h5 mate; 1...♔xg6 2.♕xf7+ ♔xf7 (2...♖xf7 3.♘e6 mate) 3.♖h7 mate) 2.♕f7+ ♔xf7 (2...♖xf7 3.♖h7 mate) 3.♘e6 mate.

Thomas Willemze

Club players, test your decision-making skills!
What would you play?

Pawn breaks, you better prepare them carefully. If they work they strengthen or liberate your game, if they don't work you may be in trouble. It's all about the right timing.

Pawn breaks can be very powerful tools to open up the position for your pieces, but should be handled with care. They are often complex and they can easily backfire. Finding the right moment is key and requires practice. You can improve these skills by regularly solving exercises and drawing the right conclusions.

Exercises

To get you started, I have selected four exercises from a game between Zala Urh (2159) and Teja Vidic (2179) that was played in the First Women's Bundesliga in Austria. The first three exercises are viewed from the white side and will teach you how to find the right time for your pawn break. In the last exercise, we will switch colours and try to crown Black's smooth kingside attack with success.

Exercise 1

position after 11...e4

Black has just closed the position by pushing her e-pawn. **Would you con-**tinue your development with **12.♗g2**, or seize the opportunity to push **12.d5** in order to **stir up the centre**?

Exercise 2

position after 15...♘b6

White can either finish her development with **16.♖fd1** or go for the central pawn break with **16.d5**. **What would you play?**

Exercise 3

position after 20...bxc6

White wants to improve her worst-placed piece and turns her attention to her dark-squared bishop. **How would you improve this piece?** With the subtle **21.♕a2** (and 22.♗a3), or would the bold **21.d5** be your choice?

Exercise 4

position after 27.♖f1

Something has clearly gone wrong for White during the last 10 moves. Her pieces are stuck in the corner and her king is under attack. It is too late for a pawn break and therefore it is time to switch sides and see if Black can finish off the game. **What would you play?**

I hope you enjoyed these exercises and that you were able to time your pawn breaks correctly. And that you also found a convincing way to mate the white king. You can find the full analysis of this game on the next pages.

Pawn breaks are often complex and can easily backfire. Finding the right moment is key and requires practice

Zala Urh (2159)
Teja Vidic (2179)
Graz 2021
Nimzo-Indian Defence, Rubinstein Variation
1.d4 ♘f6 2.c4 e6 3.♘c3 ♗b4
4.e3 0-0 5.♘e2

White prepares a2-a3 in order to unpin her knight and strengthen her control of the e4-square. This square tends to play a very important role in the Nimzo-Indian Defence.
5...c6 The principled move in the fight for the e4-square is 5...d5, but Black prefers to manoeuvre her bishop to the b8-h2 diagonal.
6.a3 ♗a5 7.c5

This move prevents Black from occupying the d5-square with a pawn.
7...d6 8.cxd6 ♕xd6 9.b4 ♗c7
10.♗b2 e5

Black wants to open up the position to exploit the fact that the white king will be stuck in the middle

Black wants to open up the position to exploit the fact that the white king will be stuck in the middle for a while.
11.g3
White rightly ignores the pawn and focuses on finishing her development.
11...e4

12.♗g2
This move was the solution to **Exercise 1**. White continues her development and brings her king to safety before taking action in the centre.
12.d5 looks really tempting, and White is indeed better after 12...cxd5 13.♘b5 ♕e7 14.♘xc7 ♕xc7 15.♗xf6 gxf6 16.♕xd5. However, Black is not forced to take the pawn and can play, for instance, 12...♕e7 instead.

ANALYSIS DIAGRAM

Black is threatening ...♖d8, and is clearly better after 13.dxc6 ♘xc6 14.♗g2 ♖d8 15.♕c2 ♘e5.

ANALYSIS DIAGRAM

We can conclude that White was right to finish her development first before considering the d4-d5 pawn break.
12...♖e8 13.♕c2 ♗f5

14.♖c1 14.b5 would be another premature pawn break distracting White from finishing her development. Black has a pleasant initiative after 14...♕d7 15.a4 ♗h3 16.0-0 ♗xg2 17.♔xg2 ♕f5.
14...♘bd7 15.0-0 ♘b6

16.♖fd1
The solution to **Exercise 2** was to open up the position with 16.d5!

before it was no longer possible. The timing is perfect, since the white king has found a safe spot and Black was ready to block the d-pawn for good. Play might continue 16...♘bxd5 17.♘xd5 ♘xd5 18.b5.

ANALYSIS DIAGRAM

The pawn break has activated most of White's pieces and even allows her to win back the pawn, since 18...cxb5 19.♖fd1 is too dangerous for Black.

16...♖ac8 Black should have taken the opportunity to block the white d-pawn for good with 16...♘bd5!.
17.b5 White realizes that she needs a pawn break to liberate her pieces on the queenside, but does not find

the right one. 17.d5! would again have been the way to go, and now 17...♘bxd5 18.♘d4 ♗g6 19.♘h3 ♖cd8

ANALYSIS DIAGRAM

20.♘xd5 ♘xd5 21.b5. Black is under pressure and is again unable to keep her c-pawn.
17...♗b8 18.♕b1 h5!

Black initiates an attack on the kingside and increases the pressure on her opponent. White really needs to activate her pieces and generate counterplay before it is too late.
19.a4 h4 20.bxc6 bxc6!
This move is far stronger than 20...♖xc6, because the pawn controls the important b5- and d5-squares.

21.♕a2
This move fails to solve White's problems. 21.d5! was still required, and the solution to **Exercise 3**. White will have decent compensation for the pawn after 21...cxd5 22.♘b5 ♖xc1 23.♕xc1 ♕e7 24.♗xf6 ♕xf6 25.♘bc3.
It is never easy to find the right timing for a freeing move like d4-d5. The complex lines following this pawn break can easily tempt you to postpone your decision. However, this move will have to be played at some point, and the best you can do is to rely on your intuition and take the plunge before you will no longer get the chance.
21...hxg3

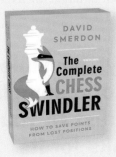

22.hxg3 ♗e6

This is the start of an elegant bishop manoeuvre, but the immediate 22...♘g4! would have been stronger. Now, after 23.d5 ♕h6 24.dxc6, Black has

ANALYSIS DIAGRAM

24...♗e6. A very instructive move. The bishop is on its way to c4. 25.♕b1 ♕h2+ 26.♔f1 ♗c4. Nothing beats an attack from different directions! The white kingside is about to be dismantled, e.g. 27.♖d4 ♗xg3 28.fxg3 ♕xg3 29.♘d1.

ANALYSIS DIAGRAM

It is mate in three! 29...♘h2+ 30.♔g1 ♘f3+ 31.♔f1 ♕e1, mate.

23.♕a1 ♗b3 24.♖e1 ♘c4

25.♘b1 ♘g4

26.♖c3 26.♗h3 would run into 26...♘xf2! 27.♔xf2 ♕h6. White is completely busted after 28.♘g1 ♕g5! 29.g4 f5.
26...♕f6 27.♗f1

27...♗d1!
A beautiful move that returns the light-squared bishop to the attack. However, this was not the only solution to **Exercise 4**. You can also be proud of yourself if you had calculated 27...♕h6 28.♖e1 ♘cxe3 29.fxe3 ♗xg3 30.♘xg3 ♕h2+ 31.♔f1 ♕xg3 32.♖e2 ♖e6! and mate cannot be prevented.
28.♘f4 28.♖xd1 ♕xf2+ 29.♔h1 ♗e6 leads to a forced mate after 30.♘f4 ♖h6+ 31.♘h3 ♖xh3+ 32.♗xh3 ♕h2 mate.
28...♗xf4 29.exf4 ♗f3 30.♖xf3

30...♕h6!
With great attacking mastery, Black completes her onslaught. Playing forcefully, she prevents her opponent from liberating her pieces and involving them in the defence.
31.♖c1 ♕h2+ 32.♔f1 exf3

White was unable to prevent mate on the next move and resigned. An impressive attacking victory by Black!

Conclusion
Pawn breaks can be powerful, but should be timed well. White was right to wait until her pieces were ready, but ended up in trouble because she postponed her decision for too long. Remember that it is not always possible to calculate the exact outcome of a complex pawn break and be ready to trust to your intuition when the position asks for it. ∎

Remember that it is not always possible to calculate the exact outcome of a complex pawn break and be ready to trust to your intuition when the position asks for it

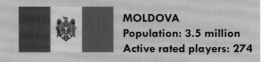
They are The Champions

The 2021 Women's Champion of Moldova is Svetlana Petrenko. Twelve players took part in the seven-round Swiss tournament from February 6 to February 14 in Chisinau. Both Svetlana and defending champion Valentina Verbin scored 6 out of 7 and tied for first place. Petrenko was declared the champion, as she was the winner of their personal encounter. The players used masks and hand sanitation, and temperatures were checked. The tournament was held just at the right time. In March, the Covid situation worsened, and all OTB tournaments were cancelled.

This is Svetlana's 13th national women's title. She won the women's title for the first time in 1993, and the Open Championship in 2005. Her victory against GM Vasile Sanduleac in the last round of the Moldova Open Championship in 2005 was one of her most memorable games. Unexpectedly for everyone, she became the champion amongst men – a unique achievement in Moldovan chess history! The realization of this success only came later, because she had to hurry to get to the train immediately after the game to travel to the next tournament, in Belgrade. During those years, Svetlana had a very tight schedule, with 10 to 14 tournaments a year.

Svetlana was a late bloomer in chess by today's standards. She was introduced to chess at school at the age of 10. Her parents took her to the local chess club, and there she was taken under the wings of Ion Solonari, a well-known Moldovan chess coach, who also trained Victor Bologan as a child. At 22, she became a Woman International Master, at 27 a Woman International Grandmaster, and at 30 she gained the title of International Master.

She generally wins her games by what she calls 'gradual suffocation'. Not in

ANDREAS KONTOKANIS, BAKU OLYMPIAD 2016

SVETLANA PETRENKO
Moldova

the game below, though! Svetlana loads Alekhine's Gun and does not hesitate to pull the trigger.

Shota Azaladze (2215)
Svetlana Petrenko (2346)
Batumi 2003

position after 32... ♕c5+

33.♔h1?! 33.♕d4 ♕g5 would have maintained the balance. **33...♖f2!** The only way to gain an advantage. **34.♕d4 ♕f5 35.♔g1 ♖f8 36.♕d1 ♕g5 37.g3 ♖xf1+ 38.♕xf1 ♕e3+** 0-1.

Svetlana has never been a fanatic about chess titles and ratings. As in her games, she improved gradually by training persistently and being mentally strong. Svetlana approaches chess as an art, loves to play, create something new, travel, and communicate. She represented Moldova at 10 Women's Chess Olympiads and at two European Championships, where she won a silver medal in the team competition (2001). Svetlana considers this her most significant success in her international chess career. Since 1992, she won or got medals in many international tournaments in Moldova, Romania, Hungary, Germany, Spain, Ukraine, Kazakhstan, Serbia, and Russia. Finally, Svetlana twice participated in the knock-out Women's World Chess Championship.

The past year, with all those Covid restrictions, has been different. Svetlana did not play a single over-the-board or online game between the two Moldovan women's championships of 2020 and 2021! It gave her a chance to spend more time on another passion, Jyotish (Vedic astrology), which she has studied for 10 years now. During the past year, she prepared horoscopes for several strong grandmasters based on detailed birth information.

On December 14, 2020, a total solar eclipse occurred in Jyeshtha Nakshatra, which predetermined the beginning of a difficult period for those born under this star, including Garry Kasparov and Donald Trump. On the day of the eclipse, during the meeting of the Electoral College, Trump lost his presidency...

In **They are The Champions** we pay tribute to national champions across the globe. For suggestions please write to editors@newinchess.com.

Kaja Snare

Studio Host Meltwater Champions Chess Tour

CURRENT ELO: 'Don't have one, hehe'

DATE OF BIRTH: February 9, 1990

PLACE OF BIRTH: Kongsvinger, Norway

PLACE OF RESIDENCE: Oslo, Norway

BARD GUDIM

What is your favourite city?
New York City.

What was the last great meal you had?
Restaurants have been restricted in Oslo since November... But I did make some tasty slow-cooked tacos the other night.

What drink brings a smile to your face?
A margarita on a roof top in NYC.

Which book would you give to a friend?
A Little Life by Hanya Yanagihara.

What book is on your bedside table?
Currently only a crossword magazine.

What is your all-time favourite movie?
Remember the Titans.

And your favourite TV series?
It's not an all-time favourite, but I did love *The Queen's Gambit*.

What music do you listen to?
Usually I just put on Top Hits in Norway on Spotify.

Is there a work of art that moves you?
I have a huge print of Diego Maradona in my living room, of the moment he won the World Cup with Argentina in 1986. It was delivered to me a few hours before the news broke that he had passed away. How strange is that!

What is your earliest chess memory?
Playing chess with my dad when I was little and how impatient it made me feel.

Who is your favourite chess player?
It was because of Magnus Carlsen I got interested in chess, being Norwegian and a sports journalist. I also often think

he plays the most entertaining games. But I could mention so many names here. Vladimir Kramnik and Vishy Anand stand out as two exceptional representatives for chess.

Is there a chess book that had a profound influence on you?
Chess or Life by Atle Grønn is fantastic for someone who loves chess but doesn't understand it.

What was your best result ever?
Landing the job at Play Magnus, hehe.

What was the most exciting chess game you ever saw?
Game 6 of the 2014 Anand-Carlsen match. All the raised eyebrows when Magnus blundered and had to hide it. And won the game.

What is your favourite square?
h2 with Simon Williams' Harry.

Do chess players have typical shortcomings?
For people with exceptional memories they can be like goldfish when they win a big tournament, and are mostly just annoyed they played a bad final game.

Facebook, Instagram, Snapchat, or?
I communicate on Snapchat and hang out on Instagram.

What is your life motto?
I don't have one, but sometimes remind myself that the journey is the destination.

Who or what would you like to be if you weren't yourself?
I'm happy with my own life, although I'm not exceptional at anything. It would

be cool to be Usain Bolt for 9.58 seconds just to feel what it is like to run that fast.

Which three people would you like to invite for dinner?
Magnus Carlsen, Garry Kasparov and Bobby Fischer. To settle the big question once and for all.

Is there something you'd love to learn?
Chess.

Where is your favourite place?
My parents' cabin up in the mountains. At dusk, the mountains turn blue, and the world is just so quiet and beautiful.

How do you relax?
Go for a run, do crossword puzzles, cook, watch sports, or play the fantastic board game Terraforming Mars.

If you could change one thing in the chess world, what would it be?
No changes, just add-ons.

What does it mean to be a chess player?
If you spend hours every day thinking about chess moves, even without a chess board, you're probably a chess player.

Is a knowledge of chess useful in everyday life?
The queen is the most powerful piece even though the king gets all the attention. Hehe.

What's the best thing ever said about chess?
How the 64 squares embrace everything from sports to science to art, combined with cultural history and global prevalence that no other game can compare with. – Atle Grønn.